About the author

This is my first attempt at writing about my early life, now that I have reached the ripe old age of eighty-two. Lockdown has given me time to reminisce.

ADOLESCENT LOVE
A Story of Young Love in the 1950s

BRIAN JOHN ROBSON

ADOLESCENT LOVE

A Story of Young Love in the 1950s

Vanguard Press

VANGUARD PAPERBACK

© Copyright 2021
Brian John Robson

The right of Brian John Robson to be identified as author of
this work has been asserted by him in accordance with the
Copyright, Designs and Patents Act 1988.

A CIP catalogue record for this title is
available from the British Library.

ISBN 978 1 80016 234 1

*Vanguard Press is an imprint of
Pegasus Elliot MacKenzie Publishers Ltd.*
www.pegasuspublishers.com

First Published in 2021

**Vanguard Press
Sheraton House Castle Park
Cambridge England**

Printed & Bound in Great Britain

Acknowledgements

Special thanks to Frances Devey, Susan Hatfield, Shirley Harman, Jenny Tustin and Rosemary Wormington, who encouraged me to write my story.

CHAPTER 1

The message appeared on my Facebook page from a Janet Palmer, which read: *I am Janet. I used to work at Kelshaw. Are you the John I knew?* An unexpected message from a past life. A lot of water has gone under the bridge since then.

Sixty-three years ago, in 1956, I fell in love with a Janet Palmer whilst working at Kelshaw. This message brought back so many memories.

The nineteen fifties were not the best of times. Families were still getting over the ravages of war. England was still rebuilding the future. We seemed to be living in a void. The promiscuous sixties were still years away. Those of us born during the war, were trying to embrace this new way of life. Young love was like sand castles, too fragile to weather a storm. It was a frustrating and emotional time, when hormones were raging and parents didn't seem to understand this new generation. Treading carefully through adolescence in the mid-fifties was not easy. I had to embrace the attitudes and restrictions imposed.

At eighty-one years old, sitting in my comfy armchair, on this grey, frosty evening, I have been reminded about those carefree days. My memory begins to become clearer. The picture of my first girlfriend, Janet, becomes imprinted in my brain. Reminiscing is one of my few remaining pleasures. Over the next two years, Janet and I communicated by email. We discussed those years together, sixty odd years ago.

I lost my wife three years ago to cancer. Janet now lives on her own following her husband's sudden, fatal heart attack one year ago. It is fortuitous that two lonely people should be reunited, even if it is only by text. Neither of us thought we would still have feelings for one another, and it is very unlikely we could rekindle that spark again, but we enjoy reminiscing.

My schooling proper commenced at the end of the war. During my early years it was rather haphazard, but the authorities knew the importance of education and some form of teaching was present throughout wartime. Teaching consisted of confining us to our desks throughout the week, learning the three Rs (reading, writing and arithmetic) with maybe one hour to go into the fields to observe nature. We also had to carry gas masks throughout the day and practise getting under our desks in case there was an air raid.

After the war had ended in 1945, school centred on the three Rs with the addition of fitness activities. Other subjects such as physics, science and biology were later added to the curriculum.

At age eleven I passed my entry exam to go the King Edward Sixth Grammar School fifteen miles away. I should have left when I became fifteen, but I only obtained three GCE O-level passes, whereas five passes were expected if you wished to get a decent job, so was persuaded to attend night school to reach that goal. This I achieved by June the following year.

It was now August 1955 and I was just sixteen. I promised myself that I would start living life to the full. Before it had been long school hours and homework. Living in my village there were few people of my age and most of those thought I was a snob because I went to a good school. I was a loner, not of my own volition, but that is how it was. I spent a lot of time kicking a football up against a wall, trying to improve my ball control skills, as there was very little else to do.

On Tuesday I decided to go for a walk over to the sports field in the next village. This was an area put aside for village activity, with a football pitch plus an area for small children, consisting of two swings and a climbing frame.

A dozen or so youths were having football practice. I stood twenty yards away behind the goal, watching and any ball that finished up in my area I tried trapping and returning to one the players. A fella, who was observing, came across and spoke to me.

"You seem to have some football skill. Come and join us." I had an enjoyable half hour participating. At the end he came across smiling.

"You know how to handle yourself. You are pretty good. How old are you?"

"Sixteen."

"I am manager of Bromsgrove Co-Op United, on the lookout for talent. Would you like to come and join us?" That was how I got to practice with the team, and a month later I was selected to play my first competitive game, against Bromsgrove Rovers Reserves, who were in a division above us. It was a hard game which we only lost 1–0. Our captain congratulated me on my performance. I also got several pats on the back. My parents wanted to come and see me play, but I thought it would make me far more nervous if they attended. They did see the match, unknown to me, until I arrived home that evening.

I wasn't the only local loner. A lad, Keith, two years older than me, was ostracised on the grounds that he was effeminate, mainly because he wore clean clothes and never seemed to get dirty. He had to suffer calls of 'poofter', 'queer' or such like. I was the only youth that would speak to him. I felt sorry for the way he was treated. We didn't share the same interests. He enjoyed reading books, whereas I only read through necessity. He spoke nicely, was always well dressed and never seemed to dirty his hands, whereas I liked messing around in scruffy clothes. I had no real alternative for the way I dressed as I came from a poor working-class family with a disabled father.

It was on a Wednesday when I got a knock on the door and Keith stood there.

"I hope you don't mind me asking you, but I have a chance of an audition to act in Bromsgrove Drama

Group's play, *Mungo's Mansions*. It will be my first time meeting those people and as I don't know anyone there, I wondered if you would come with me this evening, to give me moral support?"

"I'm sorry, Keith, acting is not my thing."

"You don't have to be involved. Just sit and listen to us. I don't feel confident enough to go on my own."

"Sorry, I sympathise, but I have no interest in drama clubs."

"They need lads. There are just too many girls" That made a 'ping' go off in my head. I needed a girl in my life and here was a crowd of them. I considered for one moment

"All right. I'll come with you, but I don't want to be involved."

This evening would be another turning point. I had a bath, scrubbed my nails, combed my hair and put on my only decent suit. I wanted girls to see me at my best.

When we arrived, I made it clear that I didn't mind helping building scenery and set painting, but I had no interest in acting.

"You are very welcome and any help would be appreciated."

Keith got the part of an Irish immigrant in the play. I, meanwhile, was surveying the room for nice, young, would-be actresses. There were two girls who looked nice. Once I got involved, I would make my move.

I spent several evenings, over the next two months, helping out backstage, but I didn't feel the time was right to ask someone out. I had no experience, not knowing the best way to approach them. Anyway, the girl I most fancied only appeared on rare occasions.

Things were beginning to happen for me. Both football and theatre filled up most of my time. Lonely hours were now a thing of the past.

I did make a half-hearted attempt to get a job, but finished up volunteering part time in the local shop. That gave me more confidence to converse with people and attempt to chat up girls. I felt that girls were starting to look at me. I felt more mature.

The drama group's next play was, *Fly Away Peter*. Rehearsals started in January for performances in March. I had taken a shine to one young lady, April, about the same age as me. She liked to dress in black or grey. I didn't realise at the time, why she preferred those sombre colours. She seemed quite reserved. She had a big bosom, which my eyes kept focusing on. She noticed on one occasion and smiled when she caught my eye, while I found myself blushing. She was auditioning for the part of Dandy, the girlfriend of Ted Hapgood. There were no young men suitable for the part of Ted, so I decided to have a go, not because I wanted to act — far from it — but to play opposite that girl. We both got the parts we wanted. They were only small parts, but we would be in each other's company most of the time. I could see she liked me, but I wasn't confident enough to make a move. I quickly flicked through the script to see if I got to kiss her. No such luck. I spoke to the play's director

"Don't you think my part requires me to kiss the girlfriend?"

"We are not allowed to change what the author wrote, so unfortunately the answer is, no. Sorry" Never mind, I tried. Anyway, I had my arm around her most of the time we were acting.

We had been rehearsing each Wednesday, for the last seven weeks, and I still hadn't plucked up enough courage to take it further. I did not have enough confidence with this girl, not wanting to do the wrong thing while I was acting alongside her.

Tonight. was first night. April was late arriving. When she did, she had forgotten her dress for the play. Unfortunately. the clothes she arrived in were not suitable, so she asked around and eventually found a suitable, colourful dress, even though it was a tight fit. When it came to her first speech, she took a deep breath, expanding her ample chest and all the buttons on the back of her dress went pop, all the way down. I quickly reached up and held the dress together for the rest of the scene. She continued as if nothing had happened. That was the night the local paper came to review the play. It was published at the weekend. We scanned the paper on the last night. The critique said the best part of the play was the exploding dress. The critic didn't enjoy the play. He felt the storyline weak. The cast thought it deserved a better review. It was such a shame for so much effort.

The play was now over and everyone had agreed to return the next day to help clear the stage. April dropped her script as people were departing. I bent down and helped her pick up the sheets. This was my opportunity. I took a deep breath and biting my lip, blurted out, "Thirsty work, play acting. Would you like to come for a drink with me?"

"I'm sorry, but I don't drink. You can walk me home if you wish, it is so dark these nights and there are few lamps." she paused then added, "If you take me home, you can have a cup of tea at my place."

That was too good an opportunity to miss.

"Of course I will escort you home." With all the script back in order, we prepared to set off. It was a cold frosty evening. Spring had not yet reappeared, winter hadn't lost its grip. It was an overcoat and scarf night.

I only had my trusty old bike to get me from place to place, so I picked it up and pushed it with April by my side. Her torch and my bike lamp lit the way. After half a mile we reached the canal bridge. Beneath was a long tunnel through which the horses dragged barges to their destinations. As they walked the canal towpath, they left their deposits, which we had to nimbly manoeuvre around along the way.

"I live on a barge down there." She pointed down the towpath. I leaned the bike up against the bridge, took the lamp off my bike and helped her down the steep-ish slope towards the canal. The full moon cast chasms of light between the trees, with the breeze making everything come alive. It was quite a walk to where her barge was moored.

"It's quite an eery walk. I don't envy you doing it on your own."

"I'm used to it. It doesn't bother me." She helped me on to the traditionally ornately painted barge and opened the wooden doors down to the galley.

I was greeted by her mother. She was dressed all in black. Had she a bent nose and a cat, she would give a good impression of a witch.

"Is this your boyfriend?" she asked April

"No. He just offered to help me home. He would like a cuppa."

Her mother turned and waved me to the benches around the side of the middle room. I went to sit down on the far cushioned bench.

"No. You can't sit there. My husband is sitting there." I stopped abruptly. I couldn't see anyone, but didn't comment. I felt a little uneasy

"Sit yourself down there." She pointed to the bench on the left. I sat down.

April didn't say a word, until she indicated in a very matter-of-fact manner, "My mother is a medium. She communicates with my father."

"I see. Is it something you believe in?"

"Of course. Father is with us most of the time."

"That's nice for you," I said looking across at the bench. The more I looked, the more I could see the bench move. I began to shiver, although the room was quite warm.

"Are you feeling cold?"

"No. Thank you. It's lovely and warm" The knowledge that someone had noticed, made me blush.

"It looks like someone has walked over your grave," April said, with a knowing look. That was it. The rest of the night I imagined all sorts of things.

Mother (I never knew her name, unless it was Mother) brought me a cup of thick black tea which tasted rather bitter. I pretended to enjoy it. I just left a few dregs in the bottom of the cup. Once I had put the cup down, Mother picked it up and swirled the remains around. She tipped the liquid on to a plate and looking back inside the cup said, "I see two loves in your life, with a third lighting the way. A black cat will change your direction. You will be the last in line."

Most of that didn't make any sense to me but I said, "Thank you. I will remember that."

"Mark my words. I know it will come true."

I didn't know how to respond. I found it unsettling. Most of the conversation that followed was mainly based around the occult, which I knew nothing about, but smiled and nodded, I hope in all the right places. Anyway, I'm sure I felt the presence of 'Dad' from then onwards.

By midnight my mind was alive to everything. I tried to suppress my anxiety.

"Sorry. I have had a nice time, but I have to go. Thank you for the cup of tea." April got up and escorted me up the stairs to the door. She bent forward. I thought it was to give me a kiss, but no, it was to flick a crumb away from my collar.

"Can't have you going home untidy."

"Thank you. I have enjoyed our evening together."

"Will I see you before we audition for the next play?" she said. I didn't know whether she wanted me to say 'yes' or 'no'

"I might be around. I'll let you know. You are a beautiful young lady and it was lovely being with you," and with that I fled up the towpath. The shadows formed by the trees kept dancing beside me. The clouds fleeting across the moon, changed their shapes from animals to people and back again. I arrived out of breath at the bridge. Scraping my shoe of horse manure on the grass, I picked up my bike, clumsily put the lamp on its bracket and raced home.

I decided there and then no more acting. No more April. I didn't think I could cope with either of them again. It took time once I was home for my heart to stop pounding.

"Did the play go well? You are back late. I was getting worried," said my concerned mother. I hadn't invited my family to see me perform as I thought it would undermine the little confidence I already had.

19

Acting was in the past. I was far too nervous and unsure. I would have to find another way to get a girlfriend.

Keith enjoyed his acting and, I believe, continued to support the drama group. I didn't see him very often. Most of the time we were both busy and had little time to chat. I now had to start concentrating on getting a job. I couldn't live like this without money. My family were not in a position to continually support me. I searched the local paper. There were a number of vacancies, but only one was suitable for me. I set about writing my CV, posting it in the nearby post box.

CHAPTER 2

I was brought up in the small rural village of Penmanor, located five miles from the nearest town, Bromsgrove. The population of around five hundred were mainly made up of elderly folk. The war had taken its toll on the younger generation.

My dad's philosophy was 'save for a rainy day' and 'only spend what you can afford', the normal Victorian attitude. I was so pleased that he had encouraged that philosophy, so I saved most of my pocket money throughout my younger years. It was now important to get some form of transport. Thankfully I had sufficient money in my Post Office savings account to buy an old second-hand Austin A40, at what I considered a reasonable price and within my budget. Unfortunately, I was underage, so my father had to teach me to drive in the local car park. When I reached seventeen, I felt confident enough to immediately apply for my driving licence. I was nervous during my test, making a couple of mistakes, but fortunately I passed first time. Ripping up my L plates gave me a great deal of pleasure.

My application for a job at Kelshaw was accepted. It was a large engineering works near Bromsgrove. I started work in early May 1956, as an apprentice, on the commercial side of the business. This provided me with the very good apprentice wage of four pounds and twenty pence a week. I was required to spend six weeks in each department, to see how the company functioned. Also, I had to attend the local technical college for an accounting course (ICWA), to enable me to get the necessary accountancy qualifications. The course was held each Tuesday and Thursday afternoon during term time

(Being an apprentice gave me exemption from National Service until I was twenty. Before 1960 all lads, with the exception of those who failed the so called 'medical', had to spend two years compulsory service with one of the armed forces.)

As I turned into the work's car park for the first time, the realisation that I was entering a new phase in my life put butterflies in my stomach. Meeting new people, having new experiences, seemed daunting. I felt anonymous in the adult world I was now entering.

My first assignment was in the personnel department, learning company rules and procedures, followed by a very relaxed time in the transport department, where nobody seemed interested in teaching me anything. I just spent my day washing cars and making out travel vouchers. The wages department was my next move. It was one side of a brown carpeted corridor, with the punch card room opposite. My job consisted of calculating hours worked, from each employee's time card, and once a week to help collect the money from the bank ready to make up the pay slips. They were routine, monotonous jobs, but I enjoyed it.

At the beginning of August, Janet Palmer started work as a punch card operator. She was the sixteen-year-old daughter of the works manager. Her father got her that job, because she left school without any qualifications. When I first saw her, she was wearing a multi-coloured blouse, white pencil skirt, with shoes to match. Looking bright and bubbly with long blonde hair, she reminded me of my gorgeous film star pin -up, Julia Foster. I had watched all her films more than once. It was that clean, innocent look that endeared her to me. Both were so much alike, in every way.

Our eyes met. She blushed, as she walked smiling down the corridor, presumably to go to the toilet. I winked. My heart skipped a beat, those butterflies returned once again. From that moment I felt I had to know her. There was strict protocol, not to converse with people from other departments, except for work purposes. From then on, we both glanced across at any opportunity.

It was the following week before I saw her close up. She had been sent to the wages department, to deal with a time card query. The smell of scented flowers wafted as she passed. She spoke to the wages clerk, who sat next to me. Standing so close, I felt her deliberately rub her dark blue woollen skirt up against my arm, discreetly so that others couldn't see. I got the feeling we were going to be part of each other's lives. Within no time she was gone. She just gave a quick glance as she passed, swirling her skirt, but didn't acknowledge me.

I had hoped she would go to the canteen at lunch times, but her father, George, expected her to go down to his office each day and either spend time talking to him, or if he was busy, his secretary Beth, who sat in the adjoining office. Beth was George's eyes and ears. She was in her early thirties. A smartly dressed woman, who was very attentive to George's requirements. She spent much of her time in the offices and manufacturing areas, so was able to pick up snatches of conversation, which she then relayed back. There were rumours that they were too close, but like most work environments, all sorts of gossip got continually spread around. George was referred to as 'Napoleon' by the shop floor workers. He was small, rotund and walked around with one hand behind his back, as if reviewing the troops. He always seemed to me, to be a nice sort of person, the times we had met. It was my job to take the completed time cards to him to countersign, before I calculated each employee's hours worked.

It was a further two weeks before Janet and I met face to face. I was required to get some documents, which had been filed in the basement. All the old documents and stationery were kept there. It was a dank, musty place with unpainted walls. There were storage racks accommodating lots of boxes. In addition, there were two wooden chairs and a table. I was sorting through the boxes, to locate the documents I needed, when Janet appeared. Today she wore tight fitting clothes, all in pale blue, that flattered her slim figure. She had been sent down to get blank punch cards.

"Can you lift one of those boxes down for me?" She pointed to the far rack. "Please. It's too high for me to reach."

I put my paperwork down on the table and went across to where she was standing. She pointed to a box. I reached up and took it off the top shelf, handing it to her. My eyes followed as she took it across to the table, putting it down. Turning, she returned empty-handed, to where I was standing. She paused, waiting for my reaction. It felt it was the right moment.

"I don't know your name. I'm John" Of course I knew her name, but I thought it was a good opening line.

"I'm Janet. My father is the works manager."

"Oh, well, I'd better behave myself then" I tried to keep eye contact, but my eyes continually dropped down to her chest. She seemed to like that, pulling back her shoulders, emphasising her perfect little breasts. I tried to avert my eyes.

"You'd better be especially nice to me, otherwise I might tell," she flirted

"I will try to be a gentleman, but you look good enough to eat" My heart skipped more than a beat. It now sounded a silly thing to say

She blushed. Looking up, she made it clear that she wanted me to kiss her. Our lips would have met, but our noses got in the way. She giggled and lowered her eyes. I moved in again and we had a soft, gentle kiss. Her breasts pressed up against me heightened the sensation. Her eyes were closed and she looked so angelic. I hadn't realised that it was her first real kiss, but as my experience was also nil, I thought we did well. I slid my hand around her back, pulling her right against my body. I could feel the warmth through her silk-like blouse. We kissed again. I could feel her heart beating, as was mine. I was aroused, but if she could tell, she didn't acknowledge it. After what seemed a lifetime, she slowly pulled away and went over to the table, collected her box, blew me a kiss and scurried back upstairs to her office.

It took me another five minutes to pull myself together and get all the documentation I needed, before returning upstairs to the office.

Jean, a plumpish teenager, who was envious of Janet for her looks and her father's influence, was renowned for being a chatterbox. She sat at the next punch station to Janet. Unfortunately, she was walking down the corridor as I appeared from the basement. She smiled as she passed. Jean was aware that Janet had only just come from down there, so she speculated wildly. When Janet had returned to her desk, she had somehow got dust marks on the back of her blouse. Jean pointed it out, before carefully wiping it off. It was an overheard whispered conversation that later gave rise to a changed and enhanced rumour, that I was responsible for a hand mark on her back.

Both Janet and I remained oblivious of the rumour. Beth got to hear it. She knew how stories got magnified, so she was discreet when she spoke to George. He was annoyed. He couldn't have rumours like that circulating the company, especially if his daughter was involved. He asked Beth to find out about 'this boy'. She reported back that, "He's a hard worker, with a good reputation. Anyway, knowing your daughter, I don't think she would allow anything like that. You know what rumours are like at this place."

George didn't mention the conversation to Janet, when they met up that lunchtime. He believed nothing had happened, but it left a lingering doubt in his mind.

When he had finished signing a few invoices, he turned to Janet.

"I hear there's a lad working here that you like."

Janet blushed. It hadn't taken her father long to find out. "Yes. He seems really nice, but we have only spoken twice." There was a considered pause. "Dad. I hope you don't mind, but I would like to have lunch with the girls. I am missing so much of the gossip."

"I don't mind, as long as you are not part of that gossip."

"Of course not. The girls would make sure that didn't happen. We just like to talk, you know girl talk."

"If that's what you want then go ahead. I've got plenty to keep me occupied."

"Thanks Dad." She kissed his forehead.

George changed the subject, "We should go down to Kent, to see Auntie Nora this Christmas. I need to know what you think?"

"Can't we stay at home this year? You could bring her up here instead. There's nothing for me down there."

"Let me think about it."

Janet sighed. She hoped for a Christmas at home. Maybe the opportunity might arise whereby I could be invited. She thought excitedly about having lots of kisses

During the following week, Janet had lunch in the canteen, sometimes sitting with the girls, but when she could make an excuse, she would come and sit with me. We had to talk about mundane things, such as last night's TV or gossip we had heard. We both felt sure the girls were listening. It was our only opportunity to spend time together. In the evening she had to wait in the secretary's office, until her father was ready to take her home. I would have loved to stay with her, but he tended to leave as soon as the working day was over. It was going to be difficult to progress our relationship.

George had worked up to his position over twenty years. During that time Janet was growing up into a beautiful young woman with her own aspirations. George felt he was still responsible for her decision making and wanted to help her find the road which gave her the least amount of heartache. He gave our situation some consideration. He would need to make his own mind up. Should he permit the relationship, or try to break it, before it became serious?

"Would you like to invite your lad to tea, this weekend? Your mother and I would like to get to know all about him"

"Yes, please, Dad. His name is John. I think you will like him." Please like him, she thought.

"All right. I'll get Beth to leave your John a note."

The next morning the note was on my desk.

John Davies. Would you like to come for tea on Saturday? Please let Janet know your answer. G Palmer.

Of course I wouldn't turn that sort of offer down. It was my chance to spend valuable time with Janet. Except for the basement, we hadn't had any time together. Unfortunately, my car was booked into the garage, to have part of the chassis welded. I wrote back.

Janet, My car won't be available, but I don't want to miss seeing you, so I can catch the bus. It will be around six o'clock before I can get there, as I am playing football in the afternoon. Just let me know the way from the bus stop. Lots of kisses. John.

Janet slipped me a note, when we met at lunch time.

John. Six o'clock is fine. The directions are, a two-minute walk from the Quinton bus stop, straight up the hill to house number 73, on the left-hand side. It's the first of six new houses. A blue Rover car will be parked on the drive xxx.

I enjoyed my football, although we were only amateurs, in the bottom tier of the Worcester League. That Saturday I got dressed in my only suit, which was dark grey, with matching winklepickers. My football kit went into my backpack. Most of the week it had rained, but today it was occasional fine drizzle. Hopefully it would brighten up. Unfortunately, it didn't. The drizzle persisted throughout the afternoon, making the pitch more like a bog.

When we played away games, arrangements were made to meet at a designated pick-up point. Three or four team members would provide the transport. We would then drive in convoy to the ground.

The match was against Rubery Rangers. Both teams had to change in the back room of the Roebuck Pub. The changing room had virtually no facilities. Various chairs were dotted around the concrete floor. Several coat hangers were nailed to the wall. Clothes were mainly piled on the back of chairs, as the home team tended to take control of the hangers. In an alcove, there were two hand wash basins and one enclosed toilet. The nearby ground was bumpy and had a large dip in one corner. It was where cattle had grazed the previous year. The unevenness made playing difficult.

The match was uneventful and finished 0–0. The access to basins was limited, so there was no way I could wash off all the mud. I cleaned myself the best I could. Had I realised beforehand that the facilities were so poor, I would have made alternative plans. My towel was now filthy. The best I could do was to put on my suit and coat and hope the Palmers didn't mind me being a bit dirty. I looked at my watch. It was five passed five. I made a dash for the bus. Thankfully they came every fifteen minutes. My thoughts keep focusing on what I should say immediately I got to the house. I was sure they would understand when I told them the circumstances.

Chapter 3

It was quarter to six when the bus arrived at the Quinton stop, so I felt confident that the two-minute walk would get me there in plenty of time. There was patchy drizzle, but smog was gradually rolling around my shoes. I shouldn't get too wet. Looking ahead, the first set of houses seemed a distance away. I checked around. Yes, I was going in the right direction. Unfortunately, Janet had misjudged the distance, which she had calculated while going to work in her dad's Rover. It was nearly half an hour before I found the house. It was two years old, in a row of six detached houses, consisting four bedrooms, a large kitchen, dining room, study, library, with two bathrooms, one upstairs and one downstairs, plus a large garden with water fountain and bird bath.

At times I had thought I was lost, but my determination to see Janet drove me on. The drizzle hadn't ceased so I was totally saturated, while getting more and more stressed. There were shimmering pools of water on the pavement, reflecting light from the street lamps. As I reached the front door, it opened. Three people stood silhouetted by the hall light, anticipating my arrival. A voice from the hallway called, "You must be John. Just look at you. Oh dear. You are soaked through."

In the circumstances, I couldn't expect anything else. What a sight I must have looked. Not the best first impression. The bright hall light showed Janet's mother Hilda, followed closely by Janet

"Don't just stand there. Come on in. You look exhausted." She paused. "I'm Janet's mother. I'm Hilda. You can call me Hilda, if you like," she said, trying to make me feel at ease.

"I'd rather call you Mrs Palmer, if you don't mind?" Hilda nodded in agreement.

"Whatever makes you feel the most at ease." She ushered me in.

"I'm so sorry. There were no proper washing facilities" trying to explain.

Janet took my hand, then released it quickly.

"You really are saturated. My poor John."

George was hovering in the background. At just over five foot, they were a similar height. Both mother and daughter were smiling, while George stood rooted to the ground, looking like a garden gnome with cigar in hand. I looked tall in comparison, being nearly six foot and well built.

Hilda and George could have been twins, they were so much alike. Both were smartly dressed. Hilda had a white and black blouse and black skirt, while George had an unbuttoned light blue shirt, with darker blue trousers. Janet in contrast, wore an off-the-shoulder ballerina style yellow dress, with shoes to match. Hilda looked me up and down

"We must get you out of those wet clothes, right now"

She hurried me past the others, to the downstairs bathroom, while I left a dripping trail of water in my wake. George nodded as I passed. I gave him a quick 'hello'. I had been introduced to him whilst I was in the personnel department, and seen him weekly when he signed my wage cards. He nodded in return

George was in his early fifties. He just missed serving in World War One, because of his age. He had served as a mechanic in the Second World War, but had not seen active service. After the war, he started at Kelshaw and worked his way up to the management position he now held.

Hilda on the other hand, had been in service most of her early working life, until she met George. He was her first and only love.

Janet was born at the start of World War Two. As an only child, she was pampered, and found she only had to flutter her eyes to get what she wanted from her father.

"Run yourself a bath. The water is hot. When you are undressed, put your clothes outside the door and I will leave some dry clothes in their place." Hilda gave the bathroom a quick look.

"Use that towel." She pointed to the rack on the right-hand side of the bath. "Bubble bath is on the side."

I tried to continue my apology as she was leaving. She turned

"There is no need to apologise. I think it is very brave of you to make all this effort on such a nasty night," she said sympathetically.

I undressed, stacking my clothes neatly, but couldn't find anything to cover my nakedness, without it getting muddy. I listened to make sure nobody was outside, before quickly placing my dirty wet clothes in a neat-ish pile on the outside of the door. I tested the water. It was nice and hot. I added a bit too much bubble bath. First, I quickly washed my hair, before tackling the rest of my body. The water was turning browner by the minute.

When I got out, I used the large warm towel on the side rail. Emptying the bath water left a brown scum around the sides and a small residue of mud at the bottom. I tried to clean the bath but couldn't find any cleaning material, so just used my hand. It didn't make much improvement so I had to give up. With my towel wrapped around me, I opened the door and took hold of the neatly stacked clothes Hilda had left for me. She had taken them from George's cupboard. There was quite a size difference between her husband and me, causing a problem. I tried the clothes. The pants were too big, so I just put on the tracksuit, which was oversized and rather short in length leaving my stomach exposed. At least I was reasonably decent. The slippers were too small, so I left the room in bare feet.

I was greeted in the dining room by all three, who gave me a quick look. George nodded approval

"You look a bit more normal now. Go and sit down at the table. You must be hungry."

Addressing Hilda, I gestured. "I tried to clean up, Mrs Palmer, but haven't made a very good job of it. The mud seems to have ingrained itself to the sides of the bath"

"It's no problem. I know what will clean it."

I was about to continue my apology, but George put two fingers to his lips, indicating there was no need for further words. Janet came over and stood next to me. Once again, her perfume intoxicated me. She looked even more beautiful backlit by the wall lights. Smiling, she touched my hand and whispered, "I'm so glad you came. It's lovely to see you. I wondered if you would make it" She leaned forward and gave me a peck on the check. Sitting down next to me she started the conversation. "Did you win?"

I shook my head. "No, we drew 0–0 unfortunately."

"Did you enjoy it?"

"It wasn't bad, except for the weather and the cleaning facilities" They sympathised once again. "I found the walk to your house from the bus stop, a lot longer than you thought. It was more like thirty minutes."

"Oh dear," she smiled, "I'm not very good at distances, especially when judging from a moving car."

Hilda arrived with a bowl of salad and a plate of spam, placing both in the middle of the already set up table. Everyone sat down and I was given the salad bowl first. I felt all eyes on me, as I took the serving spoon and fork and helped myself to some lettuce, three small tomatoes and a piece of cucumber. I then took three slices of spam from the other dish and added mayonnaise and a piece of bread and butter to complete my plate.

"Are you sure that's all you want? There's plenty to go around," said Hilda, querying the amount on my plate

"This is fine, thank you. I don't have a big appetite."

I waited until everyone had served themselves, before starting to eat. Then it happened. I noticed a small green caterpillar inside one of the lettuce leaves. It moved slightly. I went hot and cold. All eyes still seemed to be on me, so I wrapped the lettuce leaf around the caterpillar and tried to casually eat the lettuce. Nobody said anything, so hopefully they were unaware. What else could I do? If I had brought it to their attention, it would cause embarrassment and everyone would be apologising. Anyway, it went down after a few chews.

I tried to make conversation, but it's not easy, when you don't know the family, but her parents attempted to make it light-hearted. Once the meal was over, Hilda and Janet cleared the table, before going to the kitchen to wash up.

Meanwhile George took me into the study for a smoke. He got out two large cigars and offered me one.

"Thank you, but I don't smoke."

"Good thing. Such a bad habit" He paused, before continuing, "By the way, Janet is my little girl, without much experience of the outside world. If you want to see my daughter, I hold you responsible for looking after her, making sure she is protected at all times. Have you had a girlfriend before?"

"No, I haven't. You can trust me to look after your daughter."

He sounded reassured. "I am trusting you to behave like a gentleman. We all work at the same place and loose talk spreads like wildfire, so I can't afford to have any gossip, especially about you two. Only met up outside work hours. Work time means just that."

"Of course, I will respect that. My job is very important to me. I won't do anything to compromise it."

"Good. I knew I could count on you."

At this point the girls returned and George suggested we all go into the lounge and maybe play cards.

"Don't be a spoil sport, George. We can go and watch the television. Let them stay in here." That was agreed. George's black and white television had a massive twelve-inch screen, compared with my nine-inch one back home. They loved watching programmes such as *I Love Lucy* and *Lassie*.

"You have about an hour, then I will drive you home. By that time, your clothes should be reasonably dry. They are now hanging up by the fire."

"Thank you, but I can get the bus home." I didn't like the idea of that return journey

"No, no, I will take you home in the car. The weather is too bad to make that journey on foot and by bus." I breathed a sigh of relief, but not so it would be noticed

They left the room. Janet went and stood by the sofa. She patted the back of it, so I went and sat down. She moved towards me and sat on my lap, with her arms draped around my neck, her head close to mine.

"I can hear your heart beating." She kissed my forehead.

"That's because you are so beautiful. I could eat you"

"I wish you would," she whispered. She turned her head and we kissed.

Time simply flew by. It was eight o'clock when George knocked the door and waited a few seconds before entering. It wouldn't have mattered, because we were only talking about silly things at the time.

"Unfortunately, I can't take you home. The smog is too thick. You are going to have to stay the night."

"I can't put you out." I mentally crossed my fingers, hoping I could spend the night in the same house as Janet.

"First you must phone your parents, so they know where you are. Explain about the smog."

I was quite happy about that. More time with Janet. I made the call and let Mum know I wouldn't be home until Sunday, because of the bad weather.

"Dad tells me he saw about the smog on the television. Apparently, it was so thick a man was walking in front of a London bus carrying a flaming torch to light the way. I expect it is just as thick where you are. She paused, "Now make sure that you behave yourself. Be very polite. Don't let me down, otherwise it will reflect on this family."

As Janet's family were in hearing distance, I just said, "Of course I won't. Goodnight, Mum. See you tomorrow."

For the rest of the evening three of us played rummy, so I didn't have any more time with Janet. We just kept looking at each other and occasionally holding hands. Hilda was out flitting around, clearing up and sorting out my wet clothes. while we played cards. At ten o'clock Hilda and Janet took me upstairs and showed me my bedroom.

"You should by comfy in here. Pyjamas are on the pillow." She scanned the room. "We will all be turning in shortly"

Janet gave me a kiss on the cheek, before they both went downstairs. It was a few more minutes before they all came up. My bedroom was big and cosy, with a toilet and wash basin in an adjoining room. I was putting the pyjamas on when there was a knock on the door.

"I will iron your clothes in the morning. Just leave any dirty washing in the basket under the window. Have a good night's sleep. Janet's here to say goodnight," Hilda said, talking through the door.

"Thank you, Mrs Palmer. You've been very good to me. I can iron my clothes once I get home." Hilda had gone by then, so there was no reply.

"Good night, darling. Sweet dreams," Janet whispered from outside the door.

"Night, my precious. Sweet dreams." I blew a loud kiss.

After a short while, the house fell silent. My pyjamas didn't fit properly, but I decided to wear them, just in case there was a fire and I had to run downstairs. I remained as quiet as I could throughout the night, sleeping off and on. The night seemed to drag, but at least I had got another day with Janet. That thought kept going through my mind

In the morning Hilda whispered at my door, "Hello. John, are you awake?"

"Yes, thank you."

"I've ironed your clothes. They are outside the door."

I decided that this would be the best time to get washed and dressed. I made the bed and tidied up before going downstairs.

The morning was bright and sunny. No sign of last night's smog, but there was a chill in the air. Smog tended to come quickly and disappear just as fast. At least there was a roaring log fire, spitting away in the hearth, keeping the house lovely and warm. George was sitting in his armchair reading the newly delivered paper, while Hilda was frying my breakfast.

"You will have to excuse, Janet. She's still asleep. I will have to take you home after breakfast, as I have a lot of reports to finish before work on Monday."

"Please don't put yourself to that trouble, I can get the bus."

"No. I will take you home." I said nothing, but my heart sank. I'd had precious little time with Janet. Would we ever get any time together?

Breakfast was coming to an end when Janet appeared. Anticipating the car journey, she was dressed warmly, carrying a scarf and bobble hat by her side. She said she didn't want anything to eat, but in the end, ate a slice of toast with marmalade and drank a cup of coffee.

George beckoned us to the car. We both sat on the back seat. I put my arm around her and she snuggled up. She dozed on the way home, breathing quietly. The journey only took twenty minutes.

"I can't stop and see your folks, as I'm in a rush. Please give my apologies" Janet woke as I lifted her head off my shoulder and got out of the car. She followed, yawning, getting in the front seat. She opened the window and popped her head out, giving me a brief kiss on my cheek.

"I'll see you tomorrow," I said, blowing a kiss.

"Bye. Love you," she mouthed and then they were gone.

As the car disappeared around the corner, my folks came to the door.

"Afraid they couldn't stop. Her dad has a lot of work to finish, so he sends his apologies for rushing off." Mum looked at Dad and said nothing. Once we were in the house, Mum thought she should comment.

"When are we likely to meet your Janet? Does her father feel we are not up to his standard?"

"Oh, Mum. Please give it time. I'll ask her parents if she can come next weekend, if that's Okay with both of you."

They nodded. "Yes. That will be fine. Get her to stay for the whole evening, so we can get to know her."

"Her dad is very nice. He is busy, otherwise he would have introduced himself. Honest."

"I hope so. We don't want to make things difficult for you. We will be on our best behaviour, won't we, Dad?"

"We will be as good as gold."

I knew it wasn't going to be easy for them, as they were not used to mixing with what they considered the upper class. They believed there was a social class divide, which was difficult to cross.

Chapter 4

The small, rural village of Penmanor, lies between the cities of Worcester and Birmingham. They are about thirty miles in each direction, so I never had the opportunity to visit either place.

Transport was by local bus, which didn't go as far as the city. Some of the roads still had cobbles, which made the bus journey a real boneshaker, especially as our small single-deckers still had solid tyres.

The local farm had only just started delivering bottled milk. Birds would often peck the bottle tops and drink the cream floating on the surface. Previously we had a milkmaid who would deliver the milk by horse and cart. The milk would be in large churns. She would then measure and ladle the quantity of milk required into our milk jugs.

Our street lights were gas, which were manually lit and extinguished by the local lamplighter. It was another five years before a modern system was installed. There still remained the practice of the lamplighter tapping people's bedroom windows to waken them ready for work. Human alarm clocks!

I was educated in the local primary school, but at the age of eleven, my headmaster got me a place at an all boys grammar school, ten miles away. With travelling, it was an eleven-hour day. I finished up gaining five GCE certificates for maths, English language, physics, biology and science. School uniform consisted of a bright green and purple blazer, with cap to match, along with dark grey trousers and black shoes. I found the colours embarrassing and refused to wear them around the village. You would be in detention if you were seen in town without a cap, blazer and correctly tied tie.

School holidays meant I had more free time, but because I went to grammar school the lads in the village didn't want to know me, so I spent much of my time alone. I had very little knowledge of sex. In junior school I found the girls silly. They didn't play boys' games and they stood around chatting and giggling. At grammar school there was only one lesson on 'the birds and bees' and it came in our last year. It was less than informative. Somehow my year missed that lesson for some unknown reason. My biology was restricted to amoebae and such like, plus experiments with live frogs. My only sexual knowledge came from talking with the other lads in the playground and behind the bike shed. Most of what I learnt was incorrect. I found a copy of a Hank Janson erotic detective novel *Torment for Trixy*. There were black smug marks all over the tattered cover and dirty thumb marks and squiggles over pages thirteen, sixty and ninety-three, describing 'the act'. This book had been the school bible over the last so many years.

The most bizarre time was when I was just thirteen and this plump twenty-year-old girl from somewhere outside the village, just appeared from time to time. She took a shine to me and felt it her duty to teach me about life. She let me kiss her and fondle her breasts, while she fiddled around in my trousers, trying to get me aroused. I'm not sure how this started, but must admit it was a nice experience. It only happened on a couple of occasions and I haven't seen her since. I heard a rumour that the police have since apprehend her for soliciting. On the Monday lunchtime I quietly asked Janet, "Can you ask your parents if they will let you can come to my house, next Saturday for tea? I sure you will like my parents," and added, "They are a bit old fashioned. No frills, but they are good hearted."

"I'm a bit nervous, but it will be nice to meet them. I don't think my family would have any objections."

It was agreed that on Saturday, after the match, she would meet my folks. It was sunny that weekend and felt pleasantly warm. She was waiting for me when my car arrived at her house at lunchtime. She was wearing a dark purple polo neck sweater and jeans. She had her hair swept back into a pony-tail.

"Do you think this outfit is suitable for meeting your parents?"

"It's just right. You look beautiful. I know my parents will love you and that outfit"

After the match I took her to my home. She said she was very nervous to meet my family. I assured her she would be made very welcome. Mum and Dad came to the door, when they heard my car.

Both my parents were born at the beginning of the century. They had been through two World Wars. My father, James, fought in the First World War, in France. He was wounded in the leg and spent the last two years of the war back home. Mother, Phyllis, had been a housewife throughout her adult life. Both had seen a fair amount of hardship and when food was short, went without, to feed their two sons, John (myself) and David. David fell ill with polio. He died five years later. Neither really got over his death. Life had changed so dramatically since their childhood, that today's teenagers seemed very different and more outgoing, to how they remembered their young lives. They imagined Janet would be aloof and look down on them. They thought she looked down on them, but that was only in their minds. They had not caught up with the times.

"Mum, Dad, this is Janet." Both had put on their best outfits, to make a good impression. Introductions over, we had a reasonable evening. It started with a meal. A Sunday roast was put on our plates. Each plate was made up and served in the kitchen, so we didn't have any choice. Janet was given 'a smallish dinner' which was more than she normally ate. She persevered, so as not to offend, by clearing her plate.

"You enjoyed that, by the look of it? Now we've got trifle for pudding."

"That was very nice, thank you. I'm full up now. I couldn't eat another thing."

Mum always believed in three good meals a day and made sure we ate them.

"A dish of trifle doesn't fill you up."

"Mum, please. We don't all have big appetites."

"Are you sure?" she asked, looking at Janet.

"Yes. Very sure. thank you."

"No wonder you girls are just skin and bone."

I then intervened. "She is just right. She doesn't want to put on pounds." Mother thought she would leave it there and the subject was dropped. She served most of the trifle to the rest of us.

"Would you like a drink of pop, while we are having pud?"

"No, thank you. I don't drink pop."

Mother just gave me a knowing look.

"Come on. Eat up."

It had been a slightly awkward start. Mother said that Dad and I should wash up while she could get to know Janet. I didn't know what they talked about. I questioned Janet later in the evening.

"She was very nice. Just talked about bits and bobs" Whatever that meant.

We watched *The Lone Ranger* before playing cards. Janet didn't understand pontoon, so we both played with one hand. At nine o'clock we left.

In the car, on the way to her house, I questioned her again. "Well, what did you think?"

She tried to be diplomatic. "Your parents are nice. They were kind to me. They made me feel welcome. I only felt nervous at first. I hope they accepted me."

"Of course they did. First time meetings are always nerve racking. Well, that's my folks. They mean well. You'll get used to them."

I didn't want to dwell any more. I had more important things on my mind.

"How about a cuddle before you get home?" Those moments when the two of us could snuggle up and say daft things were few and far between.

On returning home I was interested to know what my folks thought. Dad said, "I like her. Not very chatty, but she's fine."

Mum had given it a little more thought. "She's very young. Beautiful. I haven't fully worked her out yet. Not at all what I expected. I thought she would talk with a plum in her mouth, but no, she spoke like we do. I imagined you would pick an arty type, with big round glasses. If you are happy, then she's fine by me. I'm not the one taking her out. Be careful. You both work together, so if you do fall out it might get awkward."

"Oh, Mum. I know whoever I fancy you will think she is not good enough."

"I know that. All mothers think like that. It's your life. I Just want you to be happy. If you're happy, then I'm happy."

50

With that, the conversation was over. I knew that the first introduction would be the most difficult. Hopefully we could now relax and get on with our lives.

The next step might be trickier. Here was Janet, with no experience of boys and me with an unsatisfactory knowledge of girls. I remembered George's talk, holding me responsible. I had no leeway for mistakes. It was not going to be easy to get the opportunity anyway. Time and opportunity were very limited. I was working hard at my studies, but thoughts of Janet kept coming into my head which made it difficult to concentrate. We didn't talk about sex very often, but it was constantly at the back of our minds. There were other things to occupy any free time.

Janet loved dancing. Growing up she loved to listen to her records and fanaticise that she was dancing on the stage. When she was six, she was sent to ballet classes, but never kept it up. Bedroom dancing was her thing, plus the odd dance with her dad at parties, on holiday and at the Chalet Country Club, to which I was introduced over the next few weeks. Before Janet and I went there with her mum and dad, we decided we needed dance practice.

Their local village hall was doing dance lessons on Friday evenings. One hour of ballroom, followed by one hour of modern. Because it had been going for four weeks, we felt it necessary to get one-to-one lessons, in the half hour before the normal sessions started. George arranged and paid for these. Ballroom was mainly attended by the over forties, while modern was aimed at a younger group. At eight o'clock the youngsters replaced most of the older group, for a modern style of music. We picked up the dances quickly. Waltz and rock and roll became our favourites.

Janet's parents began going to the Chalet Country Club for an evening meal, a dance and to watch the cabaret act. Now we had dancing under our belts, we went with them. We enjoyed a lot of time on the dance floor. Most of the evening the music was ballroom, with a rock and roll session near the end. We got a really good rock and roll routine together. Most of the people left the floor to watch us. I must admit, we had a spectacular routine. Janet's dress for the night was a blue ballerina style dress, with belted waist and an underskirt consisting of two layers of stiff netting. Her shoes had two-inch heels, which she took off to dance rock and roll. She now favoured short cut hair in the pageboy style, the latest fad. I preferred her hair long, but resigned myself to compliment any of the styles she chose.

"How much older and beautiful you look." Well, what else could I say?

George always paid for everything because he knew I didn't earn much money. As he paid for all Janet's outfits, he thought he had the right to approve what she should buy. On most occasions, Janet and her mother disagreed with his choice and ended up buying what they wanted. George gave me the odd tenner every now and again to help with my petrol costs.

One night we were rock and rolling, getting really into the swing. It was halfway through our routine, when I swung her over my shoulder and a sharp piece of underskirt caught my eyebrow. When the dance was over, I discovered my face covered in blood, dripping on to my shirt. Some got on her dress. Eyebrows tend to bleed profusely. People thought I was badly cut. Gathering around, they considered I might need stitches. George fetched the car and drove us to the hospital.

I held a large handkerchief over the cut to save the blood getting everywhere. When we arrived it was completely covered. It didn't take long before a nurse took me into a cubicle. The cut required a couple of stitches. I looked like a defeated boxer as I left the hospital. When I arrived home, my family were concerned, but very sympathetic.

Hilda decided to stop starching the underskirts, which would hopefully stop it happening again. Also, Janet had complained that the netting scratched her legs. Neither curbed our enthusiasm and we continued our routine at every opportunity.

Thankfully I was not wearing my jacket, when I was dancing, but it made me think, I must get another suit. The current one was getting shabby but was good enough for work. Janet and I found a silver-grey one which we both liked. I decided to keep it as my going out suit. It was unsuitable for work.

(Male company rules for office outfits were: dark suits, white shirts, plain ties and black shoes. No bold colours.

Female attire was more relaxed, although dress/skirt lengths had to be at least, knee length. No slacks/trousers allowed).

I decided to wear the suit when we entered a rock and roll competition being held at the University of Birmingham in October. Janet's parents came along for support. Janet was dressed all in yellow, while I wore a red shirt with my new trousers.

"You can keep your new suit at my house, if you wish. It may be more convenient if you only want to use it for competitions and visits to the Chalet."

"Thank you, Mr Palmer. That's very kind of you."

"You both need to look good. It's an important part of the competition image."

Ten couples had entered. The first round, all ten couples danced. I thought we did a good routine. Out of the corner of my eye, I could see one pair who looked particularly good, but I felt confident.

The following round we took the floor as separate couples, to perform our special routines. Unfortunately, near the end of our dance I caught my foot in her underskirt and we both went flying. Janet slid across the floor twisting her ankle, while I hit a table and was knocked senseless. It was a couple of minutes before I was steady enough to stand up. The Palmers were concerned, but we were soon feeling a lot better. Janet and I were so disappointed. We did have the opportunity to re-run our routine, but neither of us were capable of continuing. The judges had no other option but to disqualify us. Never mind. Hopefully we would have better luck next time, but circumstances changed. We did not enter any more competitions, so I used my new outfit every time we visited the Chalet or went out to other special events.

CHAPTER 5

I was glad I had a car, otherwise I would never have got to see Janet properly. It made getting to work a lot easier, even if the top speed was around forty miles per hour. That was sufficient for me. I just needed to get from A to B. I told Janet that with all my work I couldn't see her until the following Saturday. We were both disappointed, but I had to get settled into my course work. I made an excuse not to play football that weekend, which would allow me some time off from studying.

When George saw my car for the first time, he frowned, thought and then muttered, "I'm sorry to ask, but are you sure your car is road worthy?"

"My local garage has given it a full check-up and are very happy about its road worthiness." I felt it was unkind to decry my little car. "It is only the bodywork that looks a bit tatty."

"You have been driving my daughter around in that car. I should have looked it over earlier but I have been preoccupied with work. I need to be sure you and the car give me confidence. I'm sorry if it hurts your feelings, but safety is paramount."

I wasn't expecting that, so I decided to take all three shopping that Saturday afternoon to give him some reassurance. I had a nervy start, but proved I was a good, considerate driver and the car performed well. Still, it was a nerve-wracking experience, but did get George's approval.

Now I felt like an adult. Time to arrange my life so that I could see Janet Monday, Wednesday and Friday. After having tea, I would drive across to her house, arriving around seven p.m. We were able to spend time together in her bedroom, provided we left the door fully open. That was George's rule. They never came up to check on us as they knew that was sufficient deterrent. It didn't stop us kissing and having fully clothed cuddles. Mainly we listened to rock and roll records. Our favourites records were by Little Richard, Chuck Berry and Bill Haley. I was expected to leave around nine thirty p.m. on those occasions.

Tonight, the smog descended quickly, while I was driving home.

(Smog had been a problem, for quite a number of years, but this year the Clean Air Act was passed, by Parliament, to curb the use of domestic coal fires. Smog was the mixture of fog and smoke. With the onset of the colder autumn nights, it became worse. It took another two years, before smog gradually became just fog.)

I could not see more than a yard, so I had to stop. There was an eery silence, as if everyone and everything had anticipated this thick blanket. I was worried that someone might try and risk it, finishing up hitting my car. After around a minute a car passed me, going very slow. That car had fog lights, giving better illumination, so I followed his tail lights for about a mile, before the car stopped. The driver got out and came back to speak to me.

"Where are you aiming for?"

"Penmanor, near Bromsgrove," I replied

"Well, you are halfway up my drive. You better wait here until it clears." He hesitated and then said, "I don't know you, so I can't invite you in. My wife is nervous of strangers. I sympathise about your predicament. I hope it doesn't last too long."

"I understand," I replied, hoping the wait wouldn't be all night. I was starting to feel the cold. I had a rug in the boot so I got it and wrapped it around my shoulders. The man brought me a cup of tea after about half an hour, for which I was very thankful.

It was a good hour before it started lifting. It was gone after fifteen more minutes so I was able to carry on with my journey. My worried mother was waiting up for me. It was well after eleven, when I eventually arrived. I explained about the smog and how I finished up in someone's garden.

I needed to play football each Saturday afternoon and go training each Thursday, otherwise I would let the team down. We didn't have many reasonable players so it would be difficult finding a replacement if I decided to give up during the season. Next weekend we were playing at home. The weather was dry and mild, so I arranged to pick up Janet just after lunch, to come and watch. Afterwards she came back to my house for tea and to stop for part of the evening watching television. It was a lot more relaxing evening than the last encounter, but mum had short spells when she interrogated Janet about her earlier life. Janet seemed to accept that as normal, thank goodness.

She had to be home by ten p.m. week nights, but was allowed out until ten thirty p.m. at weekends. I made sure I got her home just before the deadline. Because I had cajoled Mum, prior to Janet's second visit, we had snacks laid out so that we could help ourselves. They had eaten what mother called 'a proper meal', before we arrived.

We left my house at nine p.m., giving us time to find a quiet gateway, where we would get partly undressed and enjoy being close. At first Janet was body conscious and embarrassed that I would see all her so called faults. Her body was beautiful to me. Once she accepted that, she became less nervous. We were curious about each other's bodies, but we trusted each other and that made our experiences more enjoyable. We gradually began talking about our feelings and which physical things we liked the most. The car thankfully had a good heater, so it was nice and warm for our cuddles. She had faultless, creamy white skin that looked heavenly in the moonlight. My skin was darker, making her body seem much paler. Our passion nearly got the better of us. Janet's mother had told her the facts of life, but instilled in her that pregnancy was unforgivable and she had to fight any thoughts of that nature. Thankfully we had restricted our so called lovemaking to kissing and not touching forbidden lower areas. I felt if this continued the tension would drive us apart. We had gone so far and then had to stop.

"You can't do this to me," Janet sobbed. "Please do something about it" I didn't know what to say or do.

These were such frustrating times. It would be the sixties, before society became more enlightened about sex. The pill was the changing point. Those days, if a girl got pregnant, then either there would be a shotgun wedding or the girl would be sent away from home before she began to show, staying away until after the baby was born, which would then be put up for adoption. Out of wedlock pregnancy, would bring shame on the whole family. Many girls were forced to give up their babies, they were given no choice.

Our problem was the lack of sexual knowledge. I had been told that when kissing, if you put your tongue in the girls mouth, at certain times of the month, she could become pregnant. I knew that wasn't true, but I didn't know the truth. Janet just knew the basic facts, but nothing else.

I was determined to get a book on the subject, so I went into town and popped into the library, searching the shelves for a book on the subject. I only found one book which was very juvenile. Apparently, the books which should have been available, were hidden away under the counter. You had to ask the librarian for them. I didn't have the nerve, so I came away with nothing.

I felt too embarrassed to talk to my father and I didn't know anyone I could trust to tell it straight. It was Janet's mother who solved our problem. She thought it was time that Janet knew the full facts and was ready to answer any questions.

"I can understand you are going through a lot of frustrating times. You hardly talk these days and have mood swings. I know you are very happy with John. You may not be aware but I can see your life is difficult at the moment. Here are two books on the subject. You should both read them. If you want to know anything else just come to me quietly. We don't want dad involved. I don't think he would understand. I just want you to be safe."

It was the first time Janet could remember her mother taking the lead. George tended to dominate and Hilda tended to stay quietly in the background.

That talk made all the difference to our relationship. We now knew what we could and couldn't do.

The next test was contraception. I must get up the nerve to get some. A lad in my football team had a couple for sale, but they had been used, then washed. I wasn't going to take the risk. No, I had to make the effort. I didn't want to go to town in case someone might recognize me, so I decided to go to Selly Park, on the outskirts of Birmingham to find a chemist. The first one

I came across had a lady serving so I went to find another. This time there was a male at the counter with three or four people waiting to be served. After about ten minutes the place was empty so I picked up courage and quickly went in trying to sound grown up and assured.

"A packet of condoms, please."

The chemist turned to the back shelf and brought out four boxes.

"Which of these do you want and in what size?" he remarked in a loud voice.

Just at that moment a young couple walked in. flustered I pointed to a blue box.

"Medium, please." By this time, I was bright red and sweating profusely.

"How old are you?" I was taken aback. I didn't think there was an age restriction.

"I'm eighteen," I said unconvincingly

"Any identification?" There was a giggle from the person behind. That was too much. I just turned and fled, hearing general amusement behind my back.

That weekend when I met Janet, she suddenly produced a condom. I was astounded. That was the last thing I expected.

"Mum gave them to me just in case we got over excited. I've never seen her so nice and helpful" Hilda then tried to impress on Janet, "Don't tell Dad. This isn't an excuse to go mad. You must respect yourself. Just be very careful"

"I will be careful. Promise. Thank you so, so much. We will be very sensible." She kissed her mum on the forehead.

"Any scares or problems come to me straightaway and I mean straightaway"

We both were very relieved, but very nervous. Janet beamed as she told me. "I can't believe she would talk to me about condoms. It was very embarrassing. It's the first time I have felt really close to her"

I was more sceptical. It seemed out of character for Hilda. I believed George had instructed her, but why? Why give us the means? Would they next offer us a room?

Janet's mum had told her to put a condom in her handbag just in case, while putting the box containing the other three hidden somewhere in her bedroom. I surmised that while Janet was at work Hilda would search her room to see if any had been taken. They would then know something had happened and possibly stop it in its tracks before it became a problem. That was my thinking at the time. I hadn't realised that Janet had been born out of wedlock. Neither of us knew that secret. I could not understand their logic, which seemed twisted. What was going through their minds?

Funnily enough, that weekend, we spent most of the time around Janet's house listening to records, with the occasional walk. The pressure had been taken off. We felt more relaxed. I hoped that Hilda would see the difference. Janet was noticeably more her old self. It seemed their ploy was working.

The following week we swapped books. Janet had covered each book, in brown wrapping paper, with *MATHEMATICS* written on the cover. I had carefully hidden mine at home in my secret drawer. I felt gradually George was accepting the situation and feeling happier about our relationship. Hilda seemed understanding and ready to help. She realised it was a fine line we all were treading.

We had now been celibate for eight weeks, as the right opportunity to take things further hadn't arisen. We needed to do the deed soon, but finding the right time and place never seemed to come our way. There was my car, but it was cramped on the back seat and not the right place for first time. We needed a proper bed and plenty of time. It had to be special.

On Friday my car heater decided to pack up and the garage had to send away for parts, so there was another obstacle. It couldn't be repaired until at least the following Tuesday. I was able to keep the car over the weekend, but as it was cold, having fun on the back seat, would not be on the cards.

In the meantime, I had been to have my hair cut. I remembered hearing the barber say on previous occasions, "Something for the weekend, sir?" Previously the penny hadn't dropped. After he cut my hair, he whispered. He always spoke those words softly, as if it was something illegal.

This time, I was brave enough to quietly say, "Yes. Two, please."

"A fella like you would need six."

Six it was. He discreetly placed them in my hand. That was the most expensive hair cut I had ever had.

It now meant that Janet could keep her condom in her handbag and the others could remain in her bedroom. Her family would never know if the deed had been done. It seemed unlikely we would ever be able to find the right place where we could be alone. My car seemed to be the only place. Most likely we would remain virgins for the foreseeable future. How ironic, now we had the means, but not the place.

Chapter 6

Soon, I would meet someone who would change my perspective on life.

At the end of October, Janet whispered at lunchtime, that her dad heard, "We are having an African visitor tomorrow and you will be looking after him."

"Nobody has said anything to me. You must have misheard."

"He's most likely a Zulu warrior."

"Don't be daft. This company wouldn't invite a savage. You've definitely misheard him."

"Just wait and see. You will be told tomorrow."

That gave me a sleepless night. I didn't speak any foreign languages. I'd never seen a person of colour, except in books, let alone a native. I dreamt of him with a feathered headdress, holding a spear. It was with trepidation that I arrived at work next morning.

At eight thirty, the chief executive entered the accounts office. Everyone stood up in unison and said, "Good morning, sir."

"Good morning, gentlemen. Please be seated." Everyone sat down again.

(It was acknowledged practice to stand and address any member of the board as sir)

He entered the chief accountant's office and they spoke together for a couple of minutes. The door opened and the accountant beckoned

"Davies. Will you come in here, please?"

"Yes, sir." I entered the office and was told to sit down. They remained standing. That was very unnerving.

The chief executive then explained. "Mr Davies. We have a young gentleman visiting this company for the rest of the week and as you are similar in age I would like you to show him around the company, department by department."

"Yes, sir. Is he English?"

He smiled. "I take it you have heard the rumour. No, he is from Africa. From Addis Ababa, at the foot of Mount Entoto. Have you heard of that place?"

"I'm not sure, sir. Sir, I only speak English."

"This young man goes to Oxford University. His English is impeccable. He will sign in at the personnel department around two p.m. They will call you when he arrives."

"Yes, sir."

He then turned to the accountant. "I will be addressing all personnel at twelve fifteen, prior to the lunch break." Turning back to me, he added, "You must give him every assistance. He will be with you throughout the week. Any problems, go to Mr

Rutherton." (this was my boss, the chief accountant.) He gestured to me. "You can go back to your desk now."

"Yes, sir. Thank you."

Once the chief exec had left, the office staff wanted to know why I had been called in to see the Big Boss.

"I don't fully know myself. Apparently, we are all going to be told at lunchtime."

Five minutes later, there was a tannoy message transmitted to all areas around the company. 'All personnel are required to attend a meeting in the conference room, at twelve fifteen today. Thank you.'

Around ten past twelve, everybody made their way to the meeting. There were around six hundred who attended. The chief executive addressed the employees.

"Today we have an important foreign visitor who will be staying for the rest of the week. He is coloured. He must be given the same respect you would give your colleagues" There was a low mumbling. "If I hear of anyone being disrespectful, I will discipline him. Do you understand?"

There were mutters of, "Yes, sir."

"You may go for your lunch now. Back to work at the usual time." My stomach was churning. I was not looking forward to this.

I had lunch with Janet

"What did I tell you?" she said smugly.

"That's all very well, but I haven't been told his name, what am I supposed to do with him, other than take him to each department."

"You'll find out all in good time, provided you're not his meal for tonight." She had an impish twinkle in her eye

"Yes. I was wondering about that. You would make a much more tender meal than me." We laughed.

The time until two, seemed endless. I received the call slightly early.

"Please report to personnel. You have a visitor."

On the way I went to the toilet, to tidy myself. On arrival I was introduced.

"This is Senyaka Ntlokwana." The personnel manager failed to pronounce it correctly.

"Just call me Paul. It makes life easier" He held out his hand. I paused before shaking it. "I'm quite harmless. I don't bite." He was black as ebony, wearing a beautiful silver-grey suit with pastel blue silk shirt and tie. He had one gold tooth that glistened. He looked like what I imagined foreign royalty would look like. I was taken aback. Not what I had imagined. He spoke BBC English, very posh. I looked scruffy in his presence. I considered he was not wearing suitable attire for the factory floor.

"I'll leave him in your capable hands." The manager gestured to me. During the afternoon, Paul told me that our Big Boss and his father were friends. Paul was a so-called prince. He was here to find out how industry functioned. Back home he was going to be put in charge of his company's manufacturing processes. This was his first visit to rural England and our first encounter with coloured people. They were mainly based in Oxford and London, where there were more foreigners, so much more acceptance initially. It would be another ten years before we saw the immigrants arrive in our area, with new commuter towns, like Redditch, being created.

I suggested he visit the offices this afternoon as he had a suit on. I tried to be tactful

"Maybe a suit isn't the right attire for the shop floor tomorrow. The factory can be a bit messy."

He smiled and nodded. "I will do what you suggest. I can see we are going to be good friends." I was getting to like him. Except for his colour, he was just like the rest of us.

Next day, he arrived, once again dressed smartly, but this time in a dark blue boiler suit. He asked if I thought it was appropriate. I nodded approval.

Everywhere I took him he was treated like royalty. People didn't know how to react to him. They hesitated before offering their hand. Maybe during the war, some of the older men had met coloured people, but they didn't look like Paul. He had a confident outward presence, but inwardly I suspected he was unsure, because he stood out in a sea of white faces.

I had very little to do during the visit. I took him to each department, introduced him as Paul and then left. I would go back to the accounts department and wait until I got a phone call to take him to his next appointment. He had lunch with me in the canteen, although we always had the table to ourselves. I felt uneasy that he was ostracized. He didn't outwardly seem to notice. He was given no special treatment except that he was taken to his hotel in a company car and fetched the next morning. He kept a cheery smile throughout. I was astounded when he told me, "Now I am eighteen I have to go back home where I am ceremoniously required to be circumcised."

"My God. They do that to you?" I said, sounding bewildered.

"Yes. I'm afraid they do."

I was so taken aback. He regaled me with some of his life experiences. As Africa wasn't involved in the war to any great extent, they tended to carry on with their normal lives. The more influential Africans sent their children to be educated in English universities or collages, and Paul was one of those.

Once the visit was over, it got me thinking. I talked with Janet

"He made me realise that I only know an area twenty miles wide. I've never been to Birmingham, nor London, nor been on holiday, nor seen the sea. I must save up so that I can go and see all those places. I've never been on a train and I only live one mile from the station."

It was now ten years since the end of the war. The country was being rebuilt. People were only just starting to search for other things to do. Holidays were on the agenda. Janet pondered, before saying, "I've only been on holiday twice, a week at Butlins last year and a day out to London on the train."

"At least that's two more things to add to my list," I frowned

I was now beginning to see how insignificant I was. There was more to life than what I was experiencing. I must make sure 1957 would be a different year. I was going to make changes, but in the meantime, I had no choice but go back to my current routine.

Chapter 7

It was now Monday sixth December. Janet was late coming to the canteen for lunch. Her dad had asked her to pop by his office, at the start of the lunch break. He had something he wished to tell her. Apparently Kelshaw were in the process of considering amalgamating with Garrett's of Belfast. George and the chief accountant were going to spend three days in Belfast to do a feasibility study. It was agreed that both could take their wives along. This would mean that Janet would be left on her own. Special dispensation was given to take her with them. While George and the accountant were working, the others could go shopping and see Belfast, meeting up in the evening for a drink and meal. Janet didn't want to go, but she had no option. She would be flying from Birmingham Airport on Saturday, arriving home the following Wednesday evening. Her parents had flown before, but Janet hadn't. She was feeling very unsure about the flying experience.

Understandably we were both upset at the news. We would be apart for five days. It seemed no time before the weekend arrived. We spent Saturday morning listening to records and having cuddles in her bedroom.

I said goodbye at lunchtime and made my way to my football match.

It was a hard game and I didn't have time to think about her until around five o'clock. Where was she likely to be? Was she in a queue at the airport or boarding the plane? Wherever she was, she was not with me. I felt aggrieved that I was left at home while she was going away to enjoy herself.

As we were getting changed, our captain, Josh, asked if anyone was going to the pub and on to a club afterwards. Now I was on my own I had time on my hands so I thought, why not.

"I'm at a loose end. Can I come with you?" Six of us decided we could do with a night out. We would meet up at The Feathers at seven. Nobody was concerned I was only seventeen as I looked older. Back home I made sure I had a good meal. I didn't want to drink on an empty stomach. I put on my best shirt, tie, jumper and slacks, just in case I went to a night club, but I didn't particularly want to go, as I hadn't got my girlfriend. Hopefully I would just have a couple of drinks, make them last and be home by ten o'clock.

Six of us arrived at The Feathers roughly at the same time. I was the youngest. Most were in their early twenties. Josh was already getting drinks from the bar. The room was quite full by this time. A jukebox was playing loudly in the middle of a smoke-filled room, and together with trying to talk over the music, my head began to ache.

"What do you want to drink, John? Do you want any crisps?"

"I'll just have a half of mild. Thanks."

Josh called for a pint. "We don't drink halves in here."

"Thanks. I'll get the next round."

We were all having a good laugh, joking about football and girls, when I found another pint in front of me. I hadn't realised second orders had been taken because of everything that was going on.

"I haven't finished the first one yet. I don't drink as fast as you lot. I don't drink very often, so this will have to be my last. Remember, I get the next round." Nobody seemed to be listening. I thought if I wasn't having any more to drink it was only fair to pay something towards the evening.

A lot more chatter followed. I finished off the first drink and was halfway through the second when the alcohol and the cloudy atmosphere seemed to get to me. One and a half pints and I was feeling drunk. How embarrassing. I excused myself. "Must go to the toilet." Nobody seemed to notice I was unsteady. Everyone was preoccupied. I don't think they even knew that I had left the table.

I tried to look sober as I made my way outside. The fresh cold air hit me and everything started spinning. I sat down and clasped my hands to the side of my head to steady myself. A wave came over me and I felt like I was floating, drifting skywards. The last time I had experienced that feeling was when I was in hospital, years ago, to have my tonsils outs and was given gas and air.

The next thing I knew was lying in a strange bed. A loud ringing noise woke me. My head was aching and my eyes felt heavy. Out of my half-opened eyes I could see someone standing over me. It looked like a tallish-woman wearing a green bra and pants with another hazy person in the background. The greenness of the underwear lingered in my mind. I tried to make sense of my surroundings.

"Come on, wake up. I have to get ready for work." I still was in a dreamlike state and didn't comprehend my situation. "You weren't much good at midnight, but you improved at two."

I didn't understand what was being said. I felt hands under my armpits as I was helped staggering from the room and plonked down on a cold chair.

"This will wake you up," I faintly heard through my haze

I felt this freezing cascade of water hit my body, making me gasp. It was so cold it seemed to burn me. I opened my eyes and looked down. I was naked and water from a shower was pounding down on me, in a bathroom I didn't recognise.

"Where am I? Who are you?" I said, looking at this woman who now appeared to be fully dressed.

"Don't you remember? You chatted me up and brought me home. Thanks for not remembering.

76

Anyway, no time for talking. I will be late. I'll help you get dressed and then we are off. I'll drop you at Bromsgrove Bus Station. Here, take these two tablets they will make you feel more alive."

Tablets were slid into my mouth and a glass of water put in my hands.

"Drink this. It will help the tablets go down" I drank, spilling most of it on the floor.

I was still feeling very unwell. My mind wasn't functioning. The woman started to help me dress.

"Lift up your leg. Put your foot in here." Her talking just bounced off my ears. I was being manipulated like a puppet on a string.

The next thing I knew was being marched outside. A blast of cold air hit me. I must have dozed off again. I began to realise I was being driven in a car over a bumpy road. It then stopped.

"Come on. You can't still be asleep. I'm leaving you here. Pull yourself together."

I staggered out of the car. The cold air brought me round to some degree. I saw a bench and staggered towards it. I had to sit down.

After about ten minutes I started feeling better and my mind began to function.

"Are you, all right?" a lady said. "You look very white. Been drinking. You need to sleep it off."

Reality began to dawn. Somehow, I had been somewhere outside reality. I must pull myself together and get home. My bus turned up twenty minutes later.

By that time my headache was feeling much better and I was back to some sort of normality. On the bus, the conductor asked where I was going

"That's four pence, please." Luckily, I just had a sixpence, but the rest of my money was missing. He clipped the ticket and handed it to me with tuppence change. I managed to recognise the bus stop ahead, so reached up and pulled the bell cord. The bus stopped and I got off. My legs still felt like jelly but the rest of me was functioning reasonably well. After a short walk I got to my front door, but had difficulty finding the lock with my key.

Meanwhile my parents had got up, and were making breakfast.

"Dad. Take John up a cuppa, please." Mum handed him tea in a mug.

He knocked my bedroom door. There was no reply so he went in. My bed hadn't been slept in. He returned downstairs

"He's not been home. I expect he had too much to drink and stayed with a pal."

"I hope so. I get worried when he's not where I expect him. I shouldn't be worrying about him at his age."

Looking at the clock, she said, "If he's not home by nine I will phone his football manager. I've not got anyone else's number."

Nine o'clock arrived and I was still not home. She phoned the manager who said that I was staying with friends and would be home soon. This wasn't true. He didn't know where I was, but wanted to put their minds at rest. This wasn't the first time he had taken these sorts of calls from worried mothers.

It was nearly ten when I arrived. They heard me fiddling with my key in the door.

"Where have you been? You could have phoned me. I have been really worried."

"Sorry, Mum. I meant to phone, but there wasn't a phone where I was staying."

"You look very white. A sleep will do you good."

"Do you want any breakfast? Do you need any tablets?"

"No, I'll be fine. Too much to drink. I need sleep. I'll see you later." I turned and stumbled upstairs. "Goodnight all. Sorry, good morning. See you around lunchtime." I got to bed, still feeling unsteady and fell into a deep sleep, waking up at two in the afternoon. I was feeling very hungry. I needed to come to terms with what had happened. Nothing from that night seem real. I couldn't believe it. Those things only happened in films. I needed to know where I had been. I must see if Josh could throw some light on what had happened, but I only had our manager's phone number

"Hi, Tom. John here. Can you give me Josh's number? I need to speak to him."

"You got home then. Worrying your parents. You don't need me to make your excuses."

Thank you for doing that. I'm sorry you got involved."

He then gave me Josh's number.

"Hi. It's John."

A surprised Josh replied, "Where did you get to last night? The last we saw of you was when you were going to the bog. You just disappeared. Did you go home without telling us? You could have said."

"I don't know what happened. I must have passed out. Next thing I knew I was home in bed. Sorry."

"You lightweight. You need to get some ale under your belt. Hair of the dog!"

"I can only say sorry. Sorry. Shouldn't drink on an empty stomach. Bye." I supposed a little white lie or two wouldn't hurt. I would just have to put the previous night down to experience. Throughout the day I tried to sort out what was real and what was just a bad dream.

Chapter 8

The next three days went slowly. The office seemed empty without Janet. They arrived back on the Thursday morning. I couldn't wait until lunchtime to find out all the news. She was quite a chatterbox. She spent the whole lunchtime regaling me with all the sightseeing and how invigorating she found her flying experience. Lunch was coming to an end when she asked, "What have you been up to?"

"It has been very quiet without you. I missed you. I just had a couple of drinks with the lads after the game on Saturday and was home well before ten."

"It's nice to know you missed me and didn't get up to any mischief."

"You can't get up to mischief around here. You know I've got college this afternoon," I said, looking at my watch. "I'm off now, otherwise I will be late. I've got a lot of homework to catch up with this evening so will see you tomorrow. Don't forget, we have dance lessons tomorrow night. Love you lots and lots."

"I love you too. I will be lonely without you this evening."

With that, we both went our separate ways. We still couldn't show our affection at work. We didn't want it misconstrued. George had said, "Your workplace is for work."

The next day I stuck to my normal routine. I met Janet in the evening. We went the short distance to the village hall in my car. Ballroom dancing was just about to start. Normally we walked there, but tonight I had other plans.

"Janet. How about skipping modern and spending that hour making up for lost time? I missed you so badly over this last week."

"Yes. That would be lovely."

The hour went by quickly. We got to learn the tango and refreshed ourselves with some of the previous week's routines

At eight p.m. I apologised for leaving and we went out to the car. I drove to our usual quiet spot, up a bumpy track to a tree lined field. Not the most romantic of places, but we were only there to kiss and cuddle. We had missed each other so much. It was beautiful holding and caressing each other. We got totally carried away. We took it in turns to undress. This was the first time both of us had been naked together. It seemed so natural. We lost all our inhibitions. We knew we were made for each other. Realisation hit me in the throes of passion. I had forgotten to use a condom. Freeing myself, I tried to stop. Janet just lay there with her eyes closed, with a dreamlike smile on her face. She mustn't know what had just happened. If she did, then I was sure she wouldn't be able to face her parents. I somehow managed to sort myself out without Janet realising. It was minutes before we spoke. We just lay there holding each other. It was far from perfect, in a cramped back seat, but like our first kiss, it felt it was the right place just then.

"That was so lovely. I had worried about what it would be like, but it was wonderful. I love you so much," she said with tears coming into her eyes.

"I feel the same. You are so beautiful." I left it a couple of minutes before reminding her, "You have to be home in twenty minutes. Put some makeup on and make yourself presentable. You can't go home like that, all tearful and flushed."

We got dressed the best we could in the car and then got out to finish off.

"You look fine now," I said brushing the shoulder of her jacket. The cold night air brought us both back to reality.

"I will dream about this night for a very long time."

"So will I," I said, hoping that unfortunate part of my experience wouldn't rear its ugly head. I looked at my watch. "We must go back now. Remember, we've only been dancing. I won't come in. Say I'm tired and have a bit of a headache. Oh, go to bed before they ask any awkward questions about how it went this evening."

"I'll do my best, my lovely boy. I do love you."

I drove slowly back to the house, to give us time to get back to normal. She kissed me goodbye. I waited until she had opened the door before setting off home.

"Was it a good session?" George asked looking up from his newspaper

"Yes, fine. John couldn't come in. He was tired and got a bit of a headache. I'm tired too. I'm going to bed. Goodnight." Turning, she went out of the room.

George looked across at Hilda, who got up and followed Janet upstairs. She was getting undressed when Hilda knocked quietly on the door

"Can I come in?"

"Yes. I'm just going to brush my teeth."

Hilda entered and went over to the basin, where Janet was holding her toothbrush

"Is everything, all right?"

"Yes. Fine, Mum."

"You don't seem your normal self. You haven't fallen out with John, have you?"

"No, Mum, everything is fine. It's just been a busy day and I'm tired."

"You would tell me if anything was wrong, wouldn't you?"

"Of course, Mum. There is nothing wrong. Honestly." She moved across and kissed her mum. "I'm just tired. I do love you."

"Love you too. Night, night."

"Goodnight, Mum."

Hilda turned and left the room, not fully convinced that everything was fine.

"She's okay. Just tired," she said to George. "Nothing to worry about."

I was worried. I worried on the journey home and all over the weekend. I had made a big mistake but I had hopefully realised in time, thank goodness. Everything would be fine. I was trying to convince myself unsuccessfully.

Please, please be okay, I thought to myself, as I arrived home.

"You're earlier than usual. Everything all right?"

"Yes, fine, Dad. Just tired. I'm going to turn in."

"Good. I will see you in the morning. Night, night."

That night I tossed and turned with the question 'what if' continually on my mind. It was around four a.m. when I eventually fell asleep, only to be awoken by a tap on my shoulder. It was Dad.

"Come one, wake up lazybones. Janet's on the phone."

"What time is it? Does she sound all right?"

"She sounds fine to me." He looked at his watch. "It's coming up to nine o'clock."

My heart was beating fast. It always seemed to be beating fast these days. I would be glad when everything was back to normal. I was wondering what to say, as I went quickly downstairs, dreading the coming conversation

"Hi, Janet. What's up? This is an early call." I tried to be as matter of fact as possible.

"Where are you playing football today?"

I was taken aback. "We've got a home match. The last before the new tear. Why?"

"I miss you so much. I just want to be with you and it's a reasonable day weather wise."

"That will be lovely."

"Can you pick me up ten-ish? I need something from the shops. We can have lunch out. Dad will pay and then on to your match. Afterwards I can have some time with your family, while you have a bath and get ready. Dad's invited us for a meal at the Chalet before we dance the night away."

"You have got it all worked out, haven't you? Yes. Okay. I'll be there, just after ten."

"Love you."

"Love you." I put the phone down. Not the call I expected. Maybe it would be okay, or was she waiting until we were on our own before asking the question: Did you use a condom?

I dressed quickly. Had my breakfast and a cuppa, then shoved my footy stuff in my backpack and was off.

Janet was waiting in the hallway when I arrived, smartly dressed in a pale blue two piece. Not the best to watch football in, but she looked good and that would make some of my team mates envious.

We drove into Bromsgrove and parked in one of the back streets. Most of the time we seemed to just be window shopping, with a 'do you like this' in most shops. Her dad had given her a few tenners, just in case she saw something she liked. The only items she bought were two pairs of seamed stockings and a suspender belt, which she waved in front of my face.

"Do you like it? Would it look good on me?"

I blushed. "It's lovely. Just buy it." I said, hoping she would stop embarrassing me.

After that buying ordeal we went for some lunch in a little café down a back street. We both had lettuce, tomato and egg salad with ham. It was insect free! As it was too early for me to go to the changing rooms we talked, kissed and cuddled in the front seats.

"That was such a lovely evening last night. Did you really enjoy it?" she asked.

"It was the most memorable evening of my life. I will always remember it."

"I don't know what I would have done if we hadn't had condoms."

"You're right my little Janet. You know I wouldn't let you down."

"I know you wouldn't. You're just perfect."

I felt I couldn't say anything else. Why make her anxious if nothing materialised? I could only wait until I knew, one way or another

We drove to the ground. Everyone was in high spirits. It was a match we should win as the other team were bottom of the table and we were midway. Janet sat on a bench the opposite side of the ground to where the changing rooms were located, as it was the best place to see the game. Thankfully she was well away from us. The team made fun of my pathetic drinking.

"You'll be on Babycham next time," Josh laughed

"I know. I know I deserve that."

"I can see you won't be coming out with us tonight," he said, nodding towards Janet.

"Let's hope you have better luck holding her, than you did holding your drink" The others laughed and I blushed.

All was forgotten once the match started. It was a rough game and although we won 4–0, I was kicked on the calf muscle and had to finish the match on the sideline. After changing, I limped to the car. Janet was already sitting inside.

"You going to be all right to drive?"

"Yes. I'll be fine if I take it steady."

"Your poor leg. No dancing for you this evening."

Once at my house, Janet had a cup of tea, sitting near the fire, chatting away to my parents. I left the room and made my bath ready. I had previously decided not to wash in the changing rooms but to wait until I got home. It meant that Janet wouldn't have to stand around at the ground. I had a good soak. I needed it to get rid of the aches and pains. I was still limping when I got dressed.

I wished I had another work suit. This one would soon look tatty if I kept wearing it everywhere. I was going to have to find the money for yet another one.

It took me around half an hour before I appeared downstairs. After a short chat we made our excuses and left for the Chalet. It was a pleasant evening, but after one attempt at dancing I sat down and allowed George to take Janet on the dance floor.

"How are things between you and Janet?" Hilda enquired.

"We are really good together. Why do you ask?"

"She has changed. I have noticed it more since yesterday. She has a glow I haven't seen for a long time. Has something happened?"

"No, Mrs Palmer. Nothing like that has happened. I promise you." I tried not to show I was lying.

"Thank you, John. That puts my mind at rest. I won't bring it up again."

I had no idea how nor when I would know. How long did it take to find out? I was unaware of a woman's monthly cycle. Did girls feel a baby wriggling in the stomach? I was really naive about the subject and I couldn't alarm Janet by asking her. it just meant more days of being worried.

Chapter 9

A new week and Christmas Eve was just five days away. I still hadn't got Janet a big present. I had got some small goodies but would need to go shopping tonight or tomorrow evening. It was work as usual. Everyone seemed ready for Christmas. I felt it had been a long year. Around half past ten, Beth phoned me in the accounts department.

"George wants to see you, straightaway."

"What is it about, Beth?"

"I don't know. I only know he's agitated."

I asked the accountant's permission to leave the office. George was standing by his desk, waiting.

"Close the door and sit down," He was very abrupt. "Have you been having sex with another woman?" I was taken aback.

"I have never had sex with anyone. Honest."

"I have trusted you with my daughter and I'm told you are seeing someone else behind her back."

"Whoever is telling you that is lying." I was beginning to sweat.

"I have just had a phone call from a young lady telling me you have had sex with her and she has proof."

"I don't know who would say that. It is not true. I swear" I wracked my brains to think. Who the hell would say such a thing?

George paused. He went over to the door. "Beth. Go down to reception. There's a package down there for me." He paused and turning back to me, added, "This should prove it one way or another."

We both waited, facing the door. I was sweating profusely. What was it all about?

Beth took a while before returning, handing an envelope to George.

"Was the person who delivered this still in reception?

"No, apparently it was a young lady, but she had left before I got there."

"Thank you, Beth. That will be all."

Beth turned and left the room, shutting the door behind her. George opened the envelope, revealing a photograph. "So what is this then?" He threw the photograph down on to the desk. "Take a look. I want an explanation"

The photo showed me lying naked on a bed with an unknown naked woman lying across my chest. You could see me clearly, but the woman was facing the other way. I knew what it was now.

"I can explain," I mumbled.

"It's not what it seems. Someone must have drugged me on the night out with the lads. I have several missing hours."

"What sort of excuse is that? I don't want to listen to your lies. I'm phoning the police. This woman thinks you are my son and is demanding one hundred pounds. I can't believe you are capable of this sort of thing."

"I'm not. I had nothing to do with it. I'm telling you the truth."

"I want you to wait inside the boardroom until the police arrive. I don't want you talking to anyone and I want you off the premises through the back door once they have interviewed you. The company can't afford this sort of publicity. You will not return to this building until you are asked. Do you understand?"

"Yes, but it is a big mistake. I wouldn't do such a thing."

George took hold of my arm, I was roughly ushered out into the boardroom.

"Sit down and wait here. Talk to no one. Do you understand?"

"Yes, but—" I was cut off mid-sentence.

The door slammed and I was left waiting. Everything around me seemed out of focus. What on earth was happening to me? It was too unbelievable to be true. I was shaking and my teeth were chattering as if I was freezing. After fifteen minutes, Beth came in with a hot cup of tea. She didn't say a word. She just patted my hand. I thanked her and she left. I needed that tea. It settled me down. At least Beth made me feel less anxious. It was a further half hour before the door opened and a large policeman entered. Beth shut the door after him. He sat down on the opposite side of the table from me.

"What have you been up to then?" he said in a friendly, but firm way.

"It is difficult to explain. I think I was drugged."

He put his hand up, as if to stop me. "We know what has happened. Your prospective father-in-law has briefly told me. These people have done it several times before. What idiots, but I still need you to tell me your story or what you can remember."

I explained the best I could, the sequence of events. At the end, he said that he believed me. "I want you to go home now and not talk about it to anyone. Not your parents, nor your girlfriend. You will be needed to repeat what you have just said down at the police station." I got up, my legs feeling like jelly. "We will call you to the station once we have interviewed the suspected culprits."

I slipped out through the back door and drove my car to a quiet spot so that I could get my thoughts straight. It would also give me time to come down to earth, before returning home. Only mum was in, so I made up an excuse.

"I was feeling unwell and my boss said I should go home."

Mum gave me an aspirin and a cup of tea. "Can I get you anything to eat before you go to bed?"

"No. I don't feel I could eat anything right now" I then went upstairs and got undressed for bed.

"I'll bring you up a cup of soup once you have had a good sleep. Soup will buck you up. Just shout down, if you need anything. I expect you have been working and playing too hard. That night out boozing wouldn't have helped."

I was shattered and distraught, falling into a restless sleep. I didn't sleep long and woke contemplating how I was going to deal with this situation. The policeman thankfully seemed to accept my story. Maybe he would be able to tell George that I was the innocent party. The first thing I had to do, was get in touch with Janet and tell her my side of the story. I couldn't wait, like I was asked. I had lied to her about being home by ten. I was sure she would understand I couldn't tell her about something that wasn't even clear in my mind. As Janet was likely to be at work and couldn't receive phone calls, I thought I would phone her mother instead, as she seemed a sympathetic listener.

Mum had heard me stirring, so came to the door. "Can I come in?"

"It's okay. I'm decent."

"I've got some hot soup. You'll feel better with something in your stomach." It was oxtail. It tasted lovely. I gave the bowl back to my mother, once I had finished.

"I needed that. I feel a lot better now. I'm going to get up. I've a phone call to make."

I dressed and went downstairs, trying to give the impression that everything was fine, but inside my stomach was churning. I waited until Mum was working in the kitchen, before I picked up the phone.

"Hello, Mrs Palmer. This is John. Can I have a word?" I had a tremor in my voice.

"I hear that you have got yourself in trouble."

"That's what I want to talk to Janet about. She should know my side of the story."

"Well, first of all, she is still at work and secondly, I doubt if she will be in any condition to speak to you. Her father has told her what happened. How could you do that to her? It will take some getting over."

"But it's not how it seems. I have not done anything wrong. I love your daughter with all my heart and would not do anything to hurt her."

"I will have to see how she is, when she gets home. If she doesn't ring you, then don't ring here. She will be upset enough. I don't expect you will get a call this evening."

"Just tell her I love her and she is the only one. I really do love her and there is no one else."

"I will tell her, if and when the time seems right, but I can't see it making a difference." She put down the phone.

I tried to maintain a sunny disposition for the rest of the day, so that I didn't get asked awkward questions. It was very difficult.

Presumably the policeman hadn't convinced George, that is if he ever talked to him after our meeting. I thought George would take my word for it. I felt he had let me down. Why not listen to what I had to say? What version of events would Janet be told?

I didn't get a phone call over the next two days. What could I do? I wasn't supposed to tell or contact anyone. I just hoped that Janet would find it impossible not to talk to me, even if it was just to scream and shout. I made up a story that Janet had gone away for the Christmas period with her family. I didn't know if my parents believed it but they didn't question it. Maybe they thought we had fallen out. What if it wasn't sorted by Christmas? Surely Janet knew I wouldn't do such a thing. I couldn't remember ever crying. I wanted to cry now but couldn't. Perhaps it was hereditary. My father had told me that they went through two wars and nobody cried. You couldn't afford to cry. In those days it was just a matter of survival.

Chapter 10

The situation changed dramatically on the Wednesday.
I received an unexpected phone call at home from Beth.
She sounded concerned

"I need to speak to you. Is it convenient to talk
now?"

"Yes. It's okay. I'm on my own. Is something
wrong?"

"I feel responsible for George and I think you could
be of help."

"Me? George has disowned me. I can't see him
wanting anything to do with me."

"Things can change very quickly. The situation has
changed overnight. After your interview with the police,
George decided that the three of them should go away
for Christmas, to get away from all that had happened.
George had also been told that day that he would be
responsible for the manufacturing side of the Belfast
plant, which means a lot more work and travelling." She
continued. "This would make his job far more taxing. I
had noticed he was getting stressed and annoyed too
easily. When Janet said she didn't want to go away and
needed to stay at home, an argument ensued. George got
so worked up that he had a heart attack. Hilda and Janet

panicked. Eventually an ambulance was called and he was rushed to Worcester Royal Hospital. He is in a serious but stable condition. Both Janet and her mother are in shock and disbelief." She sounded really concerned. "There are no relatives locally to help and neither can drive, so I got a phone call to see if I could give them lifts to the hospital. This is where you come in. I am not available to give much assistance. If you are willing, I think this would be a very good time to become involved."

"Yes. I want to help, if they will accept it."

"I think they will. They have no real choice. It's your opportunity to get back in their good books. Hilda is currently at the hospital, but Janet is at home resting"

"I'll go straightaway to the house. Thank you, Beth."

"I think it is the right thing to do. Best of luck. I'm on your side. I believe you."

I shouted to Mum that I had an important appointment. Picking up my keys I set off. What were my first words going to be? Would she answer the door? I had to see her. I parked on the drive and knocked the door. There was no answer. I knocked again and stepped back. I saw a face appear fleetingly at an upstairs window.

"I'm not going away until you come down" I shouted. There was still no movement, so I shouted again.

A neighbour came out when she heard all the noise. I turned to her.

"I'm trying to get Janet to hear me. Sorry for disturbing you" After a short pause there was movement in the hallway.

Janet arrived at the door, but didn't open it. She spoke through the door.

"I'm trying to get some sleep. I've been at the hospital most of the night."

"I've just come from the hospital. They asked me to pass on a message," I lied.

"Tell me what it is?" She still hadn't opened the door

"I can't tell you out here. The neighbours will hear" She opened the door halfway.

"Please let me in. It's really cold standing out here."

"You can come in, but only for a minute."

I went in.

Janet became very tearful. I put my arm around her. She tried to pull away.

"I love you. You are the most precious person in my life. There is no one else."

"What do you want? What is this message?"

"There is no message. I just have to tell you, that the police know I'm innocent and they have caught the culprits." Well, it was nearly the truth. "Look at me." I was trying to raise her tearful head to see my face. "I love you. Honestly. Truthfully. You are more than life to me."

I went to kiss her. She put up little resistance, but when our lips touched, she kissed me with such passion, then broke away shaking her head.

"You don't know how much I love you. You don't know how much pain I feel."

"I do know. I want to make it better. Please believe me. There is no one else."

"I want to believe you, but I don't know if I can."

She was wearing yellow and red polka dot winceyette pyjamas. My emotions were in turmoil. I ripped her jacket off and kissed her breasts breathlessly. Holding her tight I carefully lay her on the floor. She didn't resist when I took her pyjama trousers off. Oblivious of what I was doing I quickly ripped off my clothes and lay beside her on the floor. Both our heightened emotions made that moment so pleasurable. Neither of us thought of the consequences. We finally lay exhausted. Whatever the outcome we would face it together.

"We need a cuppa. I've never needed a cup of tea more than now." After draping her somewhat ripped pyjamas over her trembling body, I stood up and dressed. She sat up when I handed her the cup. The words tumbled out of my mouth.

"We need to talk about our future. I want to make our love known. I want us to get engaged. I know it is very early days and your family wouldn't approve, but we could secretly buy a ring which you could keep hidden until the time was right."

Her eyes glistened. Her world seemed to come alive.

"That would be wonderful. We could choose together."

"You are an angel. Thank you for believing me."

She stood up and held her pyjamas to her body. "I'd better get dressed and look at my jacket. I'll have to mend it, otherwise Mum might ask questions. I'll have to find another pair for tonight."

We were in a dream world. That dream came to an end the next day.

It was getting towards lunchtime and Janet was expecting Beth to arrive in the next half hour to take her back to the hospital. Janet phoned Beth to say I would be taking her instead. Beth smiled to herself saying, "That's lovely. He's a good boy. He's a keeper. You mark my words." Beth felt relieved that her plan had worked. It also meant she could get on with her own life.

We had some lunch before setting off. By the time we reached the hospital, we were gradually coming down to earth.

"I don't think I have caused you a problem. I think I stopped in time."

"I don't know what happened. I just don't know."

"You have got me, whatever the outcome."

"Nothing must have happened. I couldn't face my parents."

"Don't worry. I'm sure everything is fine. In fact, I know everything is fine."

"I trust you."

We were left with our thoughts.

Janet entered the side ward. Her dad was asleep with wires attaching him to a machine near to where Hilda's head was resting, semi dozing. Janet made herself known.

"How is Dad?"

"He's had a peaceful night. He seems a bit better. He is awake off and on. Isn't Beth with you?"

"No, Mum. John brought me. I believe him. We are back together."

"I hope you are not making a big mistake. Anyway, there are more important things to worry about. Is John outside?

"Yes."

"I don't think he should come in here. Tell him to go home and wait. We'll have to wait until your father is a lot better before confronting him with that kind of news."

"He's come to take you home so you can have some sleep. You must be so tired. I'll stay. Don't worry, I'll phone if things change."

"Beth can take me home."

"I told you, Mum, she's not here. Let John do it."

"All right, but it will take time for me to accept him again."

She stood up and they changed places. She kissed George gently on the cheek, turned and left the room, looking back as the door closed behind her.

I saw her leave the hospital and drew her attention by waving my arms.

"I'm told you are my chauffeur. Thank you very much. I do appreciate it. I could phone for a taxi."

"I am very happy to take you home. I sorry for all the hurt I have caused."

"Your relationship is just between you two. If you cause her any further pain, then I will get involved."

"I understand. Thank you. The situation was not what it seemed. Janet has accepted my version of events."

"Janet adores you. I have my feet on the ground. I may not be so accepting. Anyway, I will go along with it until I know otherwise. Where's your car parked?"

It was a quiet journey back to her house. She thanked me. I offered to take her back to the hospital in the evening, but she refused and said she would get a taxi. She didn't feel it right to impose on me.

"I'm quite happy to do it." She shook her head, so we said goodbye to each other.

I arrived home, as Dad came in the door.

"You had an eventful day?" I told him Janet's dad had had a heart attack and I was trying to help out.

"Oh dear. I am sorry. Can we do anything to help?"

"No, it's fine. Everything is under control."

"Well, just let us know if we can do anything"

The conversation changed to the evening meal. Afterwards I made a phone call and then went for a drive to get petrol.

Next day I didn't know what the situation was, so I decided I would try the hospital first. Through the window of the side room I could see Hilda, with a couple of fellas standing round the bed and George sitting up chatting. I wasn't going to interrupt, so made for Janet's house to see if she was awake. She heard my car as I was parking on the drive. She came out to meet me, looking worried.

"What are we going to do about yesterday? I am so worried. What if I am pregnant?"

"I'm sure you're not, but last night I phoned and got some advice from Tom, our football manager. He's married with two kids, so I thought he might be the best person to give advice. He suggested getting a bottle of gin, heating it and drinking about half. Alternatively, a very hot bath is also recommended. This is a good time now. We are on our own. I bought a bottle of gin last night. Is the water hot?"

"Yes. It hasn't been used so far today."

"Go and get in the bath and I will bring you the gin."

"Are you sure this will work?"

"He says it has a very good chance."

She went to the downstairs bathroom and started filling the bath up. I heated the gin, leaving the window open to let any fumes escape. By this time, she was sitting in the bath, looking as red as a turkey.

"It's so hot. I'm sweating."

"Drink this first."

She drank a reasonable amount, but not half a bottle, pulling a face all the time. "It tastes horrible."

"That's fine. I have got a bucket of cold water waiting outside the back door. I didn't tell you, but I have to tip the water over you."

"Oh no. What are you putting me through?" She ran into the garden, with me following. Thankfully the garden is not overlooked

"Keep still. I will tip this water over you." I picked up the bucket.

"God. Be quick about it. Is this really necessary?"

"Yes. Just stand still." I threw the water all over her. She groaned and grimaced.

"Right, go and jump in the bath again."

She ran in shivering and gently lowered herself into the hot water. She stayed there for a good minute before I told her, "Right, get out. Go outside. Just one more bucket of cold water."

"You must be joking. Not again."

"We must do it right. It'll be worth it in the end." I went and filled up the bucket. "Just be brave for another two seconds."

She screamed quietly as I threw the ice-cold water over her again. "You're cruel and callous."

"I'm trying to help you."

"Yes, I know. Girls get all the pain and you boys get off scot free."

"Unfortunately, that's life. Look at it another way. You'll laugh about it in the future."

105

"That's if I don't get pneumonia." She rushed back into the house

"Come on, it wasn't that bad." I followed her into the bathroom

"You don't know how ridiculous I feel. Get out of here and let me get dressed. You wouldn't like to hear what I'm thinking"

I made a quick exit. She came into the hall a few minutes later.

"I hope it works after all this."

"It will," I said confidently, keeping my fingers crossed.

"I don't know what will happen if it doesn't. I'm shivering."

"Just go to bed. You are swaying a bit. I will clear up everything down here. I'm sure it will be fine. I will stand by you all the way. You'll need a little sleep to get yourself sober."

When everything downstairs was put back to normal, I put the remains of the gin bottle back in my car's glove compartment and went back into the house.

"We've got away with that, thank God. No one will know what we've just been doing," I said gleefully

"We are all right now. Let's hope we can say that in a month's time."

George was discharged for Christmas and told to take things easy. Not to get stressed. It was agreed that I would not be around until George was fit again. Nothing would be said about our reconciliation. This was extremely difficult for both of us but we thought it the only option. I only hoped we never got another Christmas like this. Janet did phone me, as often as possible, but she cut the call short if she thought someone was likely to be around.

So, I was to have Christmas at home. I tried to show I was happy but inside I wasn't. My parents were pleased to have my company. They asked about George. I wanted to phone Janet but knew I couldn't. We did have a one-minute quiet call while everyone was listening to the queen's speech. After tea we had a prolonged game of Monopoly. As far as my folks were concerned, it was a pleasant family Christmas. The next two days we either had relatives and friends call in, or we went to visit them bearing gifts.

I remember that it was twenty-ninth of December when Janet approached her dad about me. He seemed to have mellowed. He had made a decision to take early retirement. Now he was fifty-one, the time was right. He realised that he had a stressful job and work was taking its toll on his health, the major reason for his heart attack. He told Janet that it wasn't her fault and gave her a kiss. It had really frightened him.

When the company recommenced at the start of the new year he informed the board. It was agreed that the deputy works manager would take over and George could retire from the end of February. In the meantime, George would work part time as soon as he was fit enough.

George did not object when Janet said we were back together again. His attitude was similar to Hilda.

"Be careful, darling. It's your life, but woe-betide-him if he lets you down"

She kissed her dad. "Thank you, Daddy. I know I've made the right decision. I know he's right for me. You have made me so happy."

We were going to see the new year in together. I was told we must have a taxi and be home by one o'clock. We were very happy about that. New Year's Eve arrived. We went to the Lacarno Dance Hall. It was packed with revellers. Everyone was in high spirits. We danced and laughed the night away. When Big Ben struck midnight, we kissed and joined hands to welcome in the new year, singing *Auld Lang Syne*. Those hours slipped by so quickly. On the way home in the taxi Janet whispered, "I think something is happening."

Whatever triggered it remains a mystery, but what a lovely start to the new year.

Chapter 11

The first work day of the new year had arrived. It had been an extended holiday. First, I had to find out about my work situation. The college course would be restarting the next Tuesday. I phoned reception.

"Can you put me through to the chief accountant, please." There was a pause. My heart was fluttering.

"Hello. Rutherford speaking."

"Hello, it is John Davies. Can you tell me what my situation is please?"

"We are having a meeting about you now. I will phone you back in a few minutes. Are you at home?"

"Yes, sir."

"Await my call then."

I seemed to wait a lifetime.

The phone rang. I paused for a second, taking an intake of breath.

"Hello. John Davies speaking."

"Hello. I said I would phone you back. We have discussed your situation and as the police are not considering any charges, we want you to restart next Monday."

"Thank you, sir. Thank you."

"There is an exercise we want you to undertake. We need you to work in Cheltenham, at our sub group. We have an accounting anomaly there that needs sorting out. You will be working with Caroline. Have you met her?"

"No, but I have seen her around the office."

"Good. I'm sending you all the details in the post tonight. It won't affect your course. You will have time off for that. Goodbye." That was short and sweet. So they didn't want me back at Kelshaw yet. Maybe they wanted me to reconsider my position. The letter arrived next day. I spoke to Mum and Dad.

"I'm going to work at our subsidiary in Cheltenham for the next few weeks to solve an accounting problem. It's only a temporary measure. I'm still employed by Kelshaw."

The exercise took two weeks to complete. Caroline was older and more experienced than me, so she made all the decisions on how we should proceed. We both shared the travelling. I drove one week and she drove the final week. It was hard work, but we got on well as a team. A new working strategy with the Cheltenham company was agreed, so that their accounts would come in line with those produced by Kelshaw.

When I finished my assignment, I returned to find my problem had been forgotten. I continued my apprenticeship as normal. Janet had stopped working at the company by this time as she had no reliable transport. She got a job as a waitress, working part time in the local café.

It was mid-January when the police contacted me again. I had to report to the local police station. I booked a half day holiday so that I could attend the next morning. On arrival I was put in a small room with a table and two chairs. It was a good half hour before anyone arrived

"I'm PC Dobbs. It's in connection with a blackmail case. You are John Davies, I believe."

"Yes. I'm John Davies"

"We might need you for this upcoming blackmail case. I think it doubtful as we have overwhelming evidence from fingerprints on the letter and photograph they sent, when they demanded money. I need you today to write a full statement of everything you can remember about that night. Take your time. As much detail as you can remember. When you have finished, sign it and give it to the desk sergeant. He will give it a quick read and if he is satisfied then you are free to go."

He left a pen and sheets of note paper. I spent quite a time wracking my brain for every bit of detail. I handed my statement over. It was approved, so I left. Back in the fresh air, I took a deep breath and hoped that my ordeal was now over.

The case was heard the following week in the Magistrate's Court. Neither George nor I were required to attend, but I went along just to listen. Because the couple had pleaded guilty to my abduction, no witnesses were called except for a police officer who detailed the offence. The judge then gave his judgement. They were given a suspended sentence for my ordeal, plus two years detention for previous offences. In the end they just got probation, which seemed strange. The policeman who had interviewed me at work, told me that they were facing more serious charges to which they were pleading not guilty and that case would be heard later in the year after the police investigations were completed. The sentence given today would be taken into consideration at the next trial.

It seemed I would never know what actually happened, but seeing the woman in the court room, jogged my memory about some of the events. She had been a temporary barmaid at The Feathers that night. She thought I looked like a possible victim, especially when she overheard something about me and the works manager. She presumed I was his son and if so, there must be a load of money in the family. She put something in my drink and left it for her boyfriend to do the rest. When I walked out and sat down, I passed out. He then must have got me into his car and taken me somewhere. The woman had turned up after her shift. I could only surmise that's what happened, anyway, I would never really know the truth.

It was now the twelfth of March. Janet's birthday was a week away. We had talked about an engagement ring, but never got around to doing anything about it. I suggested, if Janet would like to get engaged, I would speak to her dad, with the intention of making her birthday the day I would propose. Both her parents seemed happy, as were my parents, so the nineteenth would be the day.

That weekend we made a big effort to get that special ring. We spent over four hours before Janet found the ring she loved. It was more expensive than I could afford, but I knew Janet wouldn't be satisfied with second best, so I bit the bullet and happily (well, I looked happy) handed over the money. The ring needed altering as it was too large for her finger. It would be ready for collection on her birthday. The next weekend we went to pick it up. Janet tried it on. It looked lovely on her finger. She took it off and put it in the little presentation box and handed it back, for me to put in my pocket.

George wanted to make it a special occasion. He invited my family to a good local restaurant, the Pear Tree, to make the presentation. It became an elaborate affair. I would have rather Janet and I just did it quietly, but made no comment. My father thought it was a bit over the top. Mother thought George was trying to show he had money to burn.

The two sets of parents were going to meet for the first time. They remained polite and civil to one another, so as not to spoil the occasion, but there was a big gulf between their lives. At least they all made the effort.

There were hosts of red balloons with 'engagement' written on them, floating from the table.

We all put on our glad rags, ready to arrive at seven. Along with our meal, was a large bottle of champagne. Just before dessert, George stood up and embarrassed me by announcing, "John will now do his presentation to his bride-to-be."

Everyone stood up. I felt such an idiot. I took the box out of my pocket and opened it, going down on one knee, by the side of Janet and said hesitatingly, "Janet, will you do me the honour of becoming my wife?"

"Yes, please," she said, lowering her hand so that I could put the ring on her finger. She could see me hesitate, so moved her hand to make sure I selected the correct finger. Everyone clapped. She stood up, kissed me, then went around the table proudly showing off the ring.

Several waiters came to the table with a beautiful cake, with the inscription *Celebrating the engagement of Miss Janet Palmer to Mr John Davies*. We were made to cut it together as if it were a wedding cake. The waiters then started singing *Happy Birthday* to Janet. Both of us had to stand up and have a photo taken. Then one was taken of Janet alone, followed by one of all our group. This was a present from the management of the restaurant.

We were now official. I took it to mean that sex was now on the table, so to speak. If there were a mishap then a wedding date could be brought forward. No actual date had been selected. Janet considered her birthday next year would be an appropriate time. Over the next few weeks, she and her mother looked at suitable venues and perused several wedding planning books. I was consulted every now and again, but mainly the decisions were left to the girls.

I thought our relationship was gradually changing. Sex became a more frequent event. Although very enjoyable, it didn't match those rare forbidden moments we had in our early days. We were still confined to the car. Neither parent believed we would consider it before wedlock. Well, that was what I thought.

It was my idea to broach the subject of holidays to Janet. I had seen that English people were starting to go to southern Spain. When I was in town I went and got a travel brochure, looking through the pages for a suitable destination.

"How do you fancy coming on holiday with me? Just us two. A holiday abroad. I haven't seen the world other than my local area. We are now officially engaged, so that should be sufficient for our parents to agree." The week with Paul had made me determined to broaden my horizons. If Janet couldn't go, then I would see if anyone else was interested.

"I doubt if they will trust us enough," Janet said sadly.

"We can only ask." I approached her parents, thinking it unlikely.

"Would you object if I took your daughter on holiday to Spain for ten days?"

"Would you want to go alone or as part of a group?" enquired Gordon.

"Just the two of us."

Turning to Hilda, George nodded, "Yes, we see no problem. I would have been concerned had you been going with a group. You might get into trouble." Once again, I questioned the logic.

What a surprise. What a change in attitude. I must have been open mouthed. George had got a new perspective on life. He realised he had virtually lost his princess. He had to have accepted she was now a young woman, with a mind of her own. Such a big change in just three months. Wonders never ceased.

"When you make the booking, I want to see the invoice, to make sure you are having separate rooms."

I agreed and together with Janet we set about the booking. Easter was April fool's day, so we aimed to set off the following week. A travel agent recommended a ten-day coach holiday through France, arriving in San Sebastian for six nights. The other four days would be for coach travel, returning home after a five hour visit to Biarritz. Accommodation was two rooms, meals extra.

When George saw the invoice, he decided, thankfully, to make it an engagement present.

Hilda thought about the holiday. "Going to a hot country, you'll need plenty of sun cream."

Oh, and jewellery will burn your skin, if worn sunbathing. Things like chains around your neck and bracelets. You shouldn't take those."

I then questioned, "What about her engagement ring?"

"I'm not leaving that behind. That goes everywhere with me," Janet said defiantly.

"If you take it off, then put it in a safe place," said Hilda

"I will guard it with my life," Janet said, twisting the ring to make the point.

I determined then, that I would keep an eagle eye on it throughout our holiday. We then agreed to start making a list of everything we would need and go shopping the following weekend.

Chapter 12

The holiday arrived and Dad offered to lend me his old Kodak Brownie. I had hoped we would be able to have the use of George's more modern camera, but he refused on the grounds, "It is much too expensive to take on holiday. You could get sand in it, or lose it, or easily damage it," so we were left with my dad's camera and two rolls of film.

George drove us to Birmingham Coach Station, in Digbeth, to pick up our connection. As we drove through Birmingham, I thought how unkempt the back streets looked, compared to our village.

This holiday was to be a game changer for us. We were limited to two large suitcases. I needed three quarters of one case for all my things and Janet took the remainder, plus a large holdall to carry on the coach. I kept the camera on a sling over my shoulder.

The coach was a new luxury version allowing up to forty-eight passengers. Most seemed to be elderly couples. We were by far the youngest. We had been informed it was going to be a thirty-hour journey, travelling throughout the night. A toilet was located down some steps, midway along the coach, where a second exit was located. In the front, alongside the driver, was a bay where a second driver could rest. There would be two-hour toilet breaks and additional stops should anybody feel sick — apparently that was quite common on long journeys. Fortunately, no one was poorly on our coach. The driver had to make sure he reached certain destinations on time, such as the ferry crossing between Dover and Calais. Each passenger was given an inflatable headrest, which would become a pillar for sleeping. I was amazed to see how big England was and the amount of water in the English Channel. I took a photo of Janet, standing by the front wheel of the coach, to show that the tyres were six inches taller than her.

"Have a good holiday and be careful. Enjoy yourselves. Don't forget to keep your passports handy. You will need them at the borders."

"We are fine. I've got both ours safely tucked in my jacket pocket" I said in an excited voice. This was going to be the most exhilarating and terrifying ten days. A memory I was sure I would keep for ever.

We had been allocated the front two left hand seats, which gave us a great view of the scenery ahead. There were forty-four passengers on board. I held Janet's hand as often as I could, to give us both confidence. We were all in good spirits, with one passenger getting us singing *It's a long way to Tipperary*. Everyone turned and waved goodbye to the friends and family seeing us off. I waved and Janet blew kisses to her parents, until they disappeared from sight.

We had one stop before we reached Dover, for the ferry crossing. I saw the sea for the first time. It looked so big and wide. I felt sick-ish as the ferry went up and down over the waves, but it didn't affect Janet. It was then a four hour, one hundred- and eighty-five-mile motorway drive to Paris. By the time we got there, we were feeling stiff, achy and needing a pee. This was our dinner stop. The toilets throughout France became our preoccupation and caused a lot of amusement.

Dinner was in a posh restaurant in Montmartre. There was a trio of violists playing in the background. It was a French menu, so I'm not sure what some of the items were that we ate. It all looked very lavish, except for the toilet facilities. On the far side of the room there was a door concealing a so-called toilet, consisting of a bucket and very little else. The ladies had to take turns to visit a sheltered outside space, where there was a hole and two-foot marks, enabling you to position yourself. Two would stand on guard, while the third tried to negotiate the task. There was also a spade, if required.

Most of the French 'comfort' stops were at small hotels, where food was available. We travelled throughout the night. The drivers changed over around midnight, whilst still travelling at speed along a motorway. One drove, whilst the other slept. As daylight arrived, we passed several small villages, where men were riding bikes with sticks of bread perched between lap and shoulder. It looked very French. There were also numerous onion sellers on their way to market. Several stops later, where again the toilet facilities were medieval, we reached Bordeaux.

The toilets there were more modern. There was a lady sitting at the door, waiting for one-franc pieces to be handed to her. The gentleman positioned themselves in the first area, whilst the ladies trundled pass into their space, which was only behind a five-foot wall. Janet found an open cubical opposite where I was standing, so we were able to have a conversation 'mid-stream'.

Most of the time, we were watching the countryside go past, pointing out memorable sights on the way. After a tiring five-hundred-mile journey we reached San Sebastian on the Atlantic coast. I was very impressed by the deep blue sea and golden sands. I had never seen anything so beautiful. I wondered what the beach would be like. My expectations weren't disappointed.

Our hotel was outside the centre, overlooking the Atlantic Ocean, so we were lulled to sleep by the sound of waves gently washing over the sand, while the moonlight magnified the darkness. It was a fairly new hotel, with a large swimming pool, palmed gardens and ample sun beds. Hotel towels were laid out on each sun bed first thing each morning. Every day we were provided with fresh towels, rooms were cleaned and our beds made. The two single rooms turned out to be one large room with two single beds and just a curtain separating the two areas. We were able to draw back the curtain and push the two beds together. A far cosier arrangement. We found a single bed big enough to take us both. As we slept in only one bed, each morning I would untidy the sheets on the second bed to give the impression that both beds were slept in. I thought there was no need to move them apart.

During the day waiters would wander around the pool area, getting drinks and snacks for the guests. We were very impressed with the service. Drinks were very cheap. A double brandy, for example, would cost around six pence, in English currency. Waiters preferred our currency to the Spanish peseta. The hotel was owned and run by an English couple. The food was mainly what we got at home, plus the odd Spanish dish. Twice a week, in the evening, Spanish dancers were brought in to entertain us with traditional dances

We now had all the time to be alone and not worry about interruptions. Being in another country, away from family, made us very relaxed. We were now getting used to seeing each other naked. If we weren't wearing our swimsuits then we tended to wear very few clothes. Bikinis were acceptable for our hotel pool, but frowned upon down on the beach. They were gradually becoming more popular with the public and soon became acceptable as beachwear. Janet enjoyed coming out of the shower with a towel around her, but when she saw me looking at her, she would let it slip and found a great deal of amusement at how my body reacted.

"Is that for me?" she would say in a mischievous way and this would result in us making love. We made love at least once a day. It was a good job I had a plentiful supply of condoms.

I had the two rolls of film for our holiday snaps, to be viewed by our parents and friends on our return home. Thankfully one of the beach shops stocked this film, so we were able to have our own private pictures. Janet enjoyed having her picture taken. I was able to get a dozen pictures of her either topless or naked, just for my private use. I made sure they were nicely posed and not at all pornographic. Janet also took pictures of me but had to be careful not to show certain areas. I kept these pictures for several years, taking a couple with me, when I eventually did National Service.

The weather wasn't particularly hot and the sea was coldish, but it was heaven to us. We spent the days either by the pool or on the beach where there were numerous sand sculptures. The water was crystal clear. We paddled, but didn't fancy a swim. We only swam in the hotel pool. The warm tropical breeze had a different, but intoxicating smell, different to the air back home. We took all precautions in the sun, enjoying rubbing cream into each other's skin, which was getting browner by the day.

We took pleasure in being together, but there were the odd occasions when we differed. I was still at the honeymoon stage, so if we wanted to do different things, I would always give way. Every now and then I started wondering — should I make a stand?

"We haven't seen the old town yet, Jan. After breakfast we could take a wander for about an hour, before going down to sunbathe."

"It's not my sort of thing darling. You go if you want and I'll just stay around the pool until you are back."

"No. It's fine. I don't want to go anywhere without you. If you don't feel like it now. Maybe tomorrow."

"Yes. We can go tomorrow morning. I will feel more like having a walk then. Today, I am tired and just feel like lying around." I conceded. I just wanted to be by her side all the time.

The next day we didn't go for the walk I had proposed. Before I had time to mention it, she suggested. "Darling. Why don't we go to the beach and walk along the seafront, on the prom? We can see San Sebastian from there."

"Okay. If you would prefer that walk, then let's do it." She had got her own way. It was an enjoyable walk and I forgot about the old town.

"I just want you around, all the time, darling," I whispered in her ear.

She smiled, kissed me on my eyes and I was back in heaven. "I do love you. You are very precious." She didn't think she was being manipulative. I didn't care. She meant everything. In fact, I didn't notice the other times when I capitulated. She was happy and I was happy. All too soon, that idyllic stay came to an end.

On the seventh day, we set off on our journey home, stopping at Biarritz for a five-hour break. The sun was blazing and it gave us time for more sunbathing. While Janet lay dozing in her polka dot bikini (acceptable in Biarritz), I made my way towards the sea. There were large rolling waves pounding the beach. Two youths were diving through these large waves. I decided I would try. I took a running dive into the next big wave, but found myself being dragged downwards and away from the shore. I felt like a leaf blown by the wind. I'm going to die, I thought. How will they get my body home? I was being dragged deeper and further from the shore for a good minute, when suddenly I was thrust upwards, twisted backwards, then spewed back on to the beach, winded. I stood up, shaking, coughing sea water. That could have ended so differently. It made me realise that life could be taken away so quickly. It was my wake-up call. I didn't tell Janet. She was lying there day dreaming. Then I noticed. "Where's your ring?"

"It's in my purse, in the hotel room," she said, without moving her head.

"I took it off two days ago, because my fingers had swollen and it was hurting me."

I changed the subject.

"You have been lying in that position too long. You will start to burn. Turn over" I knelt down and fastened the clasp on the back of her bra.

Rolling over she concluded, "You're changing the subject. I wondered how long it would be before you noticed I wasn't wearing your ring."

"Okay. I know. I didn't notice. I'm coming to join you. Move over the towel, so I can lie down"

"You're wet."

"The sun will dry me off" We only had a hour before we had to put our clothes on and get back to the coach.

I can't remember much about the next twenty odd hours, before we arrived back in Calais. I was lost in my own thoughts. That large wave kept pounding in my head. It started me thinking about my attitude to life. I had seen George's heart attack as good luck. I hadn't thought about his and Hilda's feelings. I may have said, "I'm sorry and don't hesitate to ask me," but they were only words. I wasn't sorry and I only wanted to help when it suited Janet and myself. I also hadn't considered my own family. My house was where, these days, I just ate and slept. I couldn't remember asking them how their day went and such like. I didn't think about their feelings. All my thoughts and actions were about us.

Janet said on several occasions during our coach ride back to Calais that I was very quiet. We both had our own thoughts, but Janet was still in her bubble. It wasn't until we reached the ferry that I remembered we hadn't got any presents for our families.

"Jan, darling. We must get some presents, when we are on the boat."

"But they said don't bring any presents. Spend the money on yourselves."

"I'm sure they would be very disappointed if we didn't. Let's have a look around." For once I was determined to do what I thought was right. Maybe she was having too much her own way.

There were lots of trinkets on board, but the only appropriate gifts I could see, were a Spanish donkey and an onion seller on a bike. I thought they would be my presents.

"I'll take those for my folks and maybe a bar of chocolate. I think a bottle of wine and chocolate would be better for your family" Janet agreed.

We put them into the two separate bags we had purchased. When we were going through the English countryside, I said, "Jan, love. The first thing you must say when you see your folks is 'It's lovely to be home. I've missed you both'. They will love to hear you say that. Then you can start telling them all your news."

"Okay. I do know how to behave."

We arrived back in Birmingham, half an hour before our expected time of arrival. George and Hilda were sitting in a café on the far side of the bus station. In her eagerness, Janet forgot all that I hoped she would say. She just talked excitedly about the holiday.

We filled the car boot with our luggage and set off for home. George dropped me off first.

"Thank you for letting me take your daughter on holiday. We have had the most memorable time I have ever known."

"Thank you for looking after her."

Janet gave me a kiss and said, "It was lovely, and you were lovely." Pointing to her finger, she said, "I haven't lost it. It's still here. Our bond." Then with cheery waves they were off home.

I tried to say all the right things to my folks and added, "Thanks for being lovely parents, and putting up with me." I thought, at least I'm thinking of more than just myself.

I decided then that I would finish playing football. I wasn't enjoying it anymore. It was interrupting my life too much. The season had ended. I told the manager that I wouldn't be available for next session. He understood. "Football and girls don't mix. I hope it works out for you two. Best of luck."

That night, I dreamed about everything we had seen and felt over the last ten days and determined that holidays would be an annual event. I then remembered. I knew where the holiday snaps could be developed and printed, but what about the others? Another phase of my life was about to begin.

Chapter 13

The holiday should have cemented our relationship, but it didn't. Janet was quite content to carry on as before, whereas I felt I needed more variety in my life. We clashed about a number of things, but quickly made up because I thought our bond was unbreakable.

Back in the village I bumped into Keith. "Still doing drama?" I asked.

"Yes. We start the next play in six weeks."

"Good luck with that. It wasn't my thing, you know."

"I didn't think it was, but thank you for helping me, when I needed it."

"That's okay. Does April still go?"

"Which is April?"

"The girl who was my girlfriend in the last play."

"No. We haven't seen her recently."

"Right. Thanks for the update. By the way, I thought you would be doing National Service by now?" I said light-heartedly

"No. I got exemption."

"Lucky sod. How did you manage that?"

"The doctor wrote me a note saying I had got fallen arches.

"What's that?"

"The arches in my feet have fallen and that stops me being able to do drill."

(*Recently they have changed that, because it doesn't make any difference.*)

"I must think of that, when it comes to my time. I don't fancy wasting two years of my life. Oh, while I think about it. Did you dabble in photography, because I have regularly seen you out with a camera?"

"Yes, a couple of years ago I used to develop and print my own pictures."

A light went off in my head. Taking Keith to one side I quietly said, "You couldn't help me out, could you?"

"Of course, if I can help. You did me a good turn."

"It's a bit awkward. I have a roll of film that I need processing, but it's not the sort I can take to a shop, if you know what I mean?"

"If you can get all the developing and fixing solutions, I will find all my equipment and we can have a go."

"Thank you. That will be great. Can you write down what I need and I will get it when I take my holiday snaps to be processed?"

"Yes. No problem. I just need a dark room and we can discreetly tackle the problem."

"Thank you so much. That's taken a weight off my mind."

Keith gave me a list of what I needed to get, so next day I set off to Neilson's Photographic Shop. I got most of the stuff on the list, with the odd alternative. The shop said my holiday prints would be ready in one week. Keith said he would get everything ready for the following evening.

"I can't show you the first part of the process, as it needs to be done in the dark" He went into the pantry in his house, which was a small dark room, got the film out of my camera and wound it on to a spool, putting it inside a developing tank. He then screwed the lid on. (I won't bore you with the process.) When the film had been developed and fixed, we looked at the negatives produced. They weren't great. It could be the camera wasn't much good or the processing wasn't timed right. Anyway, Keith was only able to get four reasonable prints out, three of Janet and one of me, even if she had cut part of my head off in the taking of the picture. It took around four and a half hours. At least if the prints were poor, I had got the real thing as compensation.

Photography was not for me, I thought. I thanked Keith for his help and left with my prints and negatives. I kept mine of Janet just as a reminder, but Janet thought the one of me wasn't worth keeping.

The holiday photos, collected the following weekend, weren't much better, so maybe it was the fault of the camera and not Keith's attempt.

Funnily enough, I took up photography as a hobby six years later. I joined a photography club and finished up producing portfolios for prospective models and wedding photos. I did a lot of my own developing and printing. I found it a very rewarding use of my time.

My attitude towards work began to change. The work days now seemed to drag. It was the end of June when I had my first apprentice assessment. My college report was not good. I had gone downhill since my holiday. I hadn't put enough effort into learning. At times I would read a page then realise that I hadn't absorbed any of the detail. My effort was below the necessary standard.

It was also noticeable at work. The chief accountant was the person to review my progress and he wasn't happy. It was a month later I was informed that my training was being discontinued and I had the choice of a job as an accounts clerk or find alternative employment. I agreed to stay in accounts, but it meant that I would now be eligible for National Service.

The notification came through at the end of August. I was required to report to Litchfield Barracks a month later. After a so called medical, where we all stood in line naked and had to cough, I was deemed fit for service. Eight weeks basic training was given before being allocated a regiment. The training was intense. We had sixteen hours of hard graft every day. After training I was attached to the Argyle and Southern Highlanders. I do not know how I became part of a Scottish regiment. I had no Scottish blood in me. I spent most of my time working in the company stores.

After five weeks, I was shocked to receive a 'Dear John' letter telling me that Janet had found someone else. For the first time I cried, but now I didn't know why I was shedding tears. I'd felt over the past weeks that our relationship had got stale. Week in, week out, we were doing the same old mundane things. I had known for some time, that my love for Janet was just infatuation. We were not compatible emotionally. I had been driven by lust. The tears must be for the loss of innocence, the loss of adolescence. The acceptance that I was now an adult. We had been so preoccupied with ourselves we hadn't cultivated friends. Now we were parted, Janet was very lonely. She needed someone to replace me. It was only when I was given my first two-day pass, that I accidentally bumped into her. She looked embarrassed.

"I'm sorry for what I have done to you. Truly I am. I was very lonely and I needed someone and you weren't there."

"I'm sorry too. I have no hard feelings. We were great together, but we've grown up and grown apart. I won't ever forget you."

"I did love you. I still do, but it is different. I can't explain it." Tears came to her eyes. "I still have your ring," pointing to her chest.

"It's on the chain around my neck." Pulling it out from the top of her jumper.

"I'll take it off. You must have it. It's expensive."

"No. Keep it as a reminder of our lovely time together," I said, patting her hand. We looked at each other for a good thirty seconds, thinking about what we had and now lost.

"Goodbye. Good luck" I turned and walked away. She stood there watching me fade into the distance. That was the last time I saw her in the flesh.

Chapter 14
Jump forward sixty years

Both our lives had taken many turns.

I started to take up photography, as I have already said, plus I went back to the drama group, where I had done one play, and stayed with them for just under thirty years.

In 1964, I got married to Jennifer, and unbeknown to me Janet also got married the same year. I have been married twice. Sadly, both my wives died of cancer, the first after fourteen years and the second after thirty-two. I had been very lucky with both my wives. We were very close. It was different to my first love — it was deeper and longer lasting. I never had any children. It wasn't to be. I had kept the promise I made, that we would try and have holidays at every opportunity.

I finished work at sixty-five, after thirty years back at Kelshaw with a changed career. I restarted as a computer programmer, working up to the position of group computer manager by my retirement.

Three months ago, I received an unexpected message, that said:

I am Janet. I used to work at Kelshaw. Are you the John I knew?

Apparently, she had found me on Facebook. What had happened to her over those last sixty years? We emailed each other from that day, gradually putting together the facts. I always wondered what life had in store for her. Now I could fill in some of the missing details

In the days after I started my National Service, Janet was getting bored with her job and the lack of outside interests. Her parents had started taking extended holidays. Janet went with them initially, but soon wanted younger company. She found a lad to go out with. He was the son of one of George's friends. He was younger than Janet. They were introduced at The Chalet Country Club. He was a good dancer, so they initially got on well. She wrote my 'Dear John' letter at that time, but lost interest in the lad soon after. She found him very juvenile. She flitted from lad to lad and job to job. She was twenty-two when she decided it was time to settle down. She married the next fella she met, James. Fortunately, they remained happily married for just over fifty-four years. He was a thirty-five-year-old farm worker, who lived in a tithe cottage, on a farm near Tamworth. He died last year, leaving two grown up lads, who are now married and living away from home. Janet had helped her husband on the farm and when they had the finance, they branched out and bought a small holding, which they ran until his death. She then sold up and moved to Devon.

George took retirement to the extreme. Both on holiday and at home, he would eat, sit and sleep. With his sedentary lifestyle, he began putting on weight. This put pressure on his heart and he had a second, but this time, fatal heart attack. Hilda went downhill fast after his death and died of a broken heart, six months later.

Janet now lives in a little cottage on the edge of Dartmoor and fills her days with rambling, gardening and knitting. She bought herself a three-year-old rescue Labrador, which gave her the excuse of long daily walks. As the dark, cold nights began to draw in, Janet starting wondering whatever happened to her first love.

I was now alone. My parents had died, Dad from a traffic accident and my mother nineteen years later. She and Dad had just lived for each other. Mother drifted into dementia, which got worse. She was deemed a danger to herself, so I had no alternative but to put her in a nursing home. That was the last thing I wanted, but I wasn't in a position to be a full-time career and there was no outside help. She lived for another nine years, but at most visits failed to recognise me.

Both Janet and myself are on our own, in the latter stages of our lives. It is doubtful if youthful passion could ever be replicated. Young love had shaped our lives. It was our first glimpse into the adult world.

Is there a likelihood we might get together again, after all this time?

At the moment we both agree it might be a mistake to meet up in person.

"I still have your ring. If ever we meet, I'll let you have it back."

One day we might discuss it, but currently we are only an email away.

One thing, that for some reason, lingers in the back of my mind after all these sixty-three years, was what April's mother had predicted.

(1) I would have two loves and a third would light the way. Well, I was happily married twice and Janet did remind me of our love affair, which preceded my marriages.

(2) A black cat will change the direction of my life. I don't know about a cat, but Paul did make me think about my life and the possibilities that the big wide world had to offer.

(3) I will be last in line. Well, I didn't have any children, so I was the last in my family line.

I'm not sure if I am now a believer, or whether if it were said to anyone, they could find circumstances to fit the predictions. What do you think?

Printed in Great Britain
by Amazon

18533801R00080